Jay Ramsay is the author, co-auth  forty books of poetry and non-fic (2009), *Soul of the Earth: the Au* (2010), *Gita* (2012), *Monuments (2* *mond Cutters: visionary poets in America .... (......—...... —......)*, 2016), and *Dreams Down Under* (2017). *The Poet in You* (2009) publishes part of his Chrysalis poetry correspondence course, which has been running since 1990. He is a UKCP-accredited psychotherapist with individuals and couples, also running personal development groups and workshops with many years' experience in Britain and abroad.

Praise for Jay Ramsay:

Jay Ramsay is one of our most eloquent and passionate visionary poets, someone who knows that the highest role of poetry in a catastrophic time is to keep the flames of spirit burning steadily.   Andrew Harvey

What an outpouring ... packed full of fine things!   Ted Hughes

An unlocker of imprisoned souls, and true healer ... a great gift to our world and the generation who are seeking for spiritual consciousness
Kathleen Raine

So much good work!   Robert Bly

Full of life, and awe, and grace   Jeni Couzyn

He reaches inward, and love's lyrical voice sounds behind what is personal. It is the ultimate theme in all Jay Ramsay's writing ... his voice is generous and authentic.   Paul Matthews

A courageous attempt to communicate spiritual truth at a time when few poets dare to do so.   Helen Moore

He has lifted the lid on the purpose of poetry; to shed light upon the dark plac-es of the soul, to celebrate life and to help us be better people.
Anna Saunders

Fine poetry that touches the soul   Bel Mooney

Also by Jay Ramsay:

poetry
Psychic Poetry: a manifesto
Raw Spiritual: selected poems 1980–1985
Trwyn Meditations
The White Poem (with Carole Bruce)
THE GREAT RETURN books 1–6:
The Opening / Knife in the Light: a stage-poem / The Hole /
In the Valley of Shadow: a cine-poem-cum-fantasy / Divinations / Heart of Earth
transmissions
Strange Days
Journey to Eden (with Jenny Davis)
For Now (with Geoffrey Godbert)
Improvisations
Stories Beyond Words
Meditations on the Unknown God
Tantrika: love songs of the Sixth Dalai Lama
Out of This World
Midnight Silver
like lightning inside lightning
Kingdom of the Edge: selected poems 1980–1998
Alchemy of the Invisible (with Genie Poretsky-Lee)
After Rumi
The Message (with Karen Eberhardt Shelton)
Chinese Leaves / Dream Whispers (with Genie Poretsky-Lee)
The Heart's Ragged Evangelist: love poems for the greater love
Local Universe: poems written in the Stroud Valleys
Out of Time: selected poems 1998–2007
Anamnesis: the remembering of soul
Gita: a dialogue of love and freedom
Agistri Notebook
Monuments
Dreams Down Under: celebrating Australia
Hafod-Y-Llyn Notebook

anthologies (editor)
Angels of Fire: anthology of radical poetry in the 1980's
Transformation: the poetry of spiritual consciousness
Earth Ascending: an anthology of living poetry
Into the Further Reaches
Soul of the Earth: the Awen anthology of eco-spiritual poetry
Diamond Cutters: contemporary visionary poets in America and Britain (with Andrew Harvey)

non-fiction
The Poet in You
Alchemy: the art of transformation
Crucible of Love: the alchemy of passionate relationships

translations (with Martin Palmer)
Tao Te Ching
I Ching: the shamanic oracle of change
Kuan Yin: the 100 quatrains
The Book of Chuang Tzu
Shi Jing: book of history
The Three Kingdoms

for dear Pete
the first copy

Pilgrimage
a journey to Love Island

with great brotherly love
& thanks —

Jay
18.4.18
The Woolpack
Slad

Jay Ramsay

AWEN

Stroud

First published in 2018 by Awen Publications
12 Belle Vue Close, Stroud GL5 1ND, England
www.awenpublications.co.uk

Copyright © 2018 John Tekarthon Ramsay

John Tekarthon Ramsay has asserted his right in accordance with the
Copyright, Designs and Patents Act 1988 to be identified as the
author of this book

Front cover image: *Maclean's Cross, Iona*
© Kirsty Hartsiotis

Cover design: Kirsty Hartsiotis
Editing: Anthony Nanson

ISBN 978-1-906900-54-0

For Valerie Denton, Sheila Holloway,
and in memoriam Ann Wetherall,
founder of the Prison Phoenix Trust

You shall know the truth, and the truth shall set you free
Gospel of John

Home is where the heart does not have to hide
Gabriel Bradford Millar

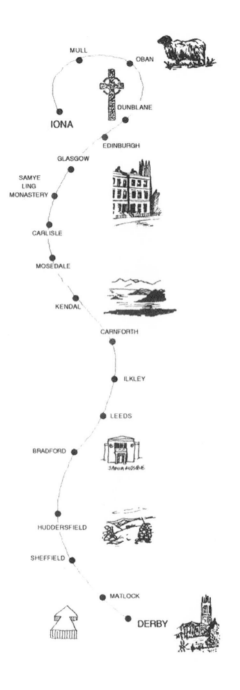

MULL

OBAN

IONA

DUNBLANE

EDINBURGH

GLASGOW

SAMYE
LING
MONASTERY

CARLISLE

MOSEDALE

KENDAL

CARNFORTH

ILKLEY

LEEDS

BRADFORD

JAMIA MOSQUE

HUDDERSFIELD

SHEFFIELD

MATLOCK

DERBY

Contents

Foreword

Jay Ramsay is a being seeking to configure, just like you and me. The job of the poet is to stand in the ever-mounting rubble of global Babylon and rage and weep and sing. To take the severed wings of the butterflies and turn them into birds. We are healers and thieves.

We only ever get glimpses of poets: they show us one tear at a time, one pond, one cage, one hill. It's a dance around what cannot be named, it's all about how far we can *not* go, and so we deceive, we beg, but really we never get there, we never arrive; our journey is ever unfinished.

Pilgrimage is a rare glimpse into what is never finished. For me, it is an odyssey. The beginning and the end are seemingly incidental and I love the way he refuses to be daunted by normality; it is as if he never eats. He doesn't seduce; he walks ahead of us: we never really see his face and it is strange and beautiful how everything he passes comes into colour, into focus – is born.

And I ran along after him and listened as he changed the colour of the sea and broke down doors.

Peter Owen Jones

Putney Bridge, London – Ilkley Moor

A sheet of rain falling over the blocked city,
Streaming, silver-grey ... as we drive to the bridge
Bumper to bumper, in line, and we wait at the lights:
It pours down vertical over the old church clock tower
With its gold hands and blue face – blue and gold –
At two o'clock – blue sky and gold –
Rising into its weathervane, by a white flagpole –
While the pink and grey squares of a high-rise office block
Loom behind it and over it, against the sky, as if bombed;
And the rain is no song, no one thanks it for falling,
For cloaking us in its soft grey cleansing calm.
Only the trees dance to it as if half-asleep in the wind.

It begins in grey: we arrive early
And sit watching the messy TV screen of the street
Through the windscreen ... and I reach for your hands,
Ahead of parting, our palms touching in silence
As we say a prayer to grow closer as we are
Where we'll meet in the spaces between by candlelight
And the love between us now will reach across all distance;

Love, and your human face, your unique face
Love, and you open my heart as you leave
And your first and last gift to me is there
As I shoulder the green boulder of this rucksack
And the moment takes our prayer in soft forgetting;
What speaks in my mind looks out through my eyes
                              and back at you, waving ...

So here's the first step – inside the coach station

I wander the length of it looking for LEEDS,
Then a sea of faces around it, waiting to board;
We queue, inch by inch, slowly straining to get in,
A sea of faces in fear that we won't, a sea of slaves,
Everyone asleep on their feet, everyone in fear
Until you loosen it up from the back then, brother.
The driver asks where you're going, you say 'Keighley',
You haven't reserved a seat, and you don't care.

Then, as we stand, the blind part us like a sea
And we all turn: she with her rucksack and white stick
And he behind her, holding her back, as they pass …
It is dark, and they are going the whole way.

Make me open to You, and Your entering into me
I don't know who I am, only what I'm seeing
I am lost in You, and only at moments
Can I see Your Face in yours, or yours, your smiling eyes

The rest is grey, the rest is waiting
The rest is pain, the rest is tears

And we pull out into the streets …

'Lord Jesus Christ have mercy on me, a sinner,' I hear
As I deepen into the voice of the unknown pilgrim
With nothing but his heart, his dry bread and starets
As he blends in his sackcloth ashes into the green.

I glance up out of the window; I misread the sign:
St Anthony's United Reformed Church becomes *Beloved* Church,
United Beloved Church – Beloved, Beloved –
There is only one church and it is Love –
One church, one temple, one synagogue, one mosque

And all the world's grey problems are this:

That we are living on a planet we have forgotten ...
And in the seat beside me an old boy with a youthful face,
Open-necked check shirt and iron-grey hair
Flaps through the pages of the *Daily Mail*.
As the newsprint catches at the corner of my eye
And he folds the paper down in his lap
I sit with my hand poised to write ... we talk
And he tells me about the War with his gentle bright eyes:
The dreams – the illusions – the rationalisations,
What it was like to be told to 'go in', and going *strange*,
His word, *strange* ... I see him dreaming, lost, uncertain,
Dreaming as I see him now, his eyes
With their watery strange blue, as clear awake as air.
'I'm seventy-eight,' he adds, and we talk on about everything,
Then slowly lapse back into silence.

Slowly, greyness greens ... in centuries
Slowly the greyness greens, for as long as it takes,
And the cloud-grey over us outside says, '*Look inside.*
The problem is you – the problem is you.'

The packed slow artery of the road
                    the broken white lines of cars racing ahead:

May a dream be with each driver, a dream like a seed
Invisibly planted by Your Hand ...

Catching a glimmer of two birds flying together,
Two becoming three, in a mobile triangle ...
Cows grazing the grass – the early gold of a harvest field
And the whitebeam in the wind turning their leaves inside out ...

And now a distant spire moving above them
Along the skyline, like a compass point, between three pylons

Till it closens round adjacent to the road –
Vanishing among the rows and rows of council houses;

But somewhere distant is the sun.
Slowly the whole land rises and the air lightens,
The green side of the field is sun
                    and the cloud's sheer is mountain.

As we slow to see the land, we slow to walking pace,
To the detail of the barley, the different grasses,
The white wayside flowers … and tree by tree under the sun
We are slowed to the earth, *slowed down to earth*
And past the black scaffold rig where the miners go down

And now rain again, spraying the big front windscreen …

As the Prayer passes from his lips into silence
And he walks and waits on the mercy of the world –

Jolted out of sleep, or a half-sleep, to find *we're there*,
Everyone's standing, landed, reaching up for their bags
And gathering outside the luggage locker –
And when I turn you're there. 'Where you going?' 'Ilkley.'
The station's this way and you're a stop before me.
'What's your name?' 'Riff.' (What a brilliant name!)
As we cross the street, laden in step,
It's a musical name in your quick Yorkshire mouth

And as we stand on the slow train, boring
Through a tunnel of green encircling the tracks,
Out towards the Moor spreading high above the town,
You talk about the hope and faith we need today,
Sporting your Greenbelt Festival hat, and I feel
The spark of this accumulating in your veins
You leave me with, like an electric quivering
As the rubbery doors clunk, and you're gone …

4

I stand waiting for the blue bus. Sing on,
Sing on in your silence ... and now it's come.

Your Welsh face and permed curls greeting me, Gilli,
And I bundle in, and we make the short drive
Out of town up to the modern retreat lodge.
Myddleton Lodge: yes, Thomas – but not the playwright.
The family were all devout Catholics
Who have sculpted this place into a living icon.

It's like a campus building as we get down
And I follow you in through the stiff swing doors
To the prefab dining hall where you're all eating,
All ten of you, eleven of us so far in this company,
Quiet over your salad and quiche, glancing up:
Tom (*Tom Pilgrim* to me), and 'This is John' (Linton)
– namesake in his ancient summer jacket – 'Hullo!'
Frederica with her fiery red Elizabethan hair
And roving Restoration eye ... 'Smyly' (David) the doctor –
And yes, he sure does smile, in his grey jacket and tie;
Josephine, with her river of Hindu silver ...
Bahai Gilli (you know), and Gwynneth (I don't –)
To whom I'm drawn to sit facing as the names all go ...

You talk about your afternoon on the Moor,
Frederica and John, senex and courtesan –
And the swastika on a rock you found, shaped like a starfish,
As the sun outside breaks through the cloud ...
And you laugh at him, with him, as he laughs at himself
Proudly declaiming his virility like Pan as he
Dances with his walking stick between the tussocks of grass
– you danced, John old man, you danced –
And after seventy years man and boy (Mr Yeats)
'Never have I ...', he didn't, but you did, like a miracle,
An old man dancing like a boy in the sun.

And after we gather briefly in the chapel to meet
In the silence as we are … you read out your prayer
That moves me to the depth of you, in the Red of Yes, sister,
As its phrases hang in the warmth that palpably emanates
Like heat, ghosting the air, where we draw breath
Meeting your eyes, one by one, as we open them …

In the gold of the evening light gathering outside
You suggest a walk to the Calvary … and we follow
The path in a loose line towards the woods
Past the Roman altar crudely carved in grey stone
With its blood-dripping hollow, like a flogging post;
Then the scent of rhododendron leaves, mauve blossoms,
With the smell of the rain earth … as we closen
To the door marked in italic by a low wooden fence
You open, and we pause at the damp threshold;

And the sun glints through the leaves, dappling, warming
Over the Angel holding the cup in the garden –
And You died for the love of this, for the love of the green,
Lord, for the love of the earth – as I follow
To where the branches shadow around you, hanging in stone,
Between two scales, and where she stands at the base
On the edge of a mountain, with her hands spread open,
Her face raised: Mary, Mother, Magdalene

And inside – your agony in chapters of stone
Set about the path it's hard to sequence –
You say, 'They make a Latin Cross …' as we wander
Among their Gothic figurine clusters and I wonder
What You would think of this now? And what do you?
Is it still like this? Or is it over?

I walk up to the altar enclosure
Under its ragged mound of ivy-covered rock, like a folly,
Where a stone on the ground has split open beside it

And where the wooden cross has tilted sideways
Among dry sticks, twists of weed, privet, and bluebells
Offered in clumps and jars … and I make my own offering,
Turning a piece of bramble into a circle, *Your Crown*,
And placing an equal-armed cross in the centre.

And as I turn, and sit, where the crucifix stone has split,
I see it in the trees, the sunlight and the blue, rising
This is Your Resurrection – in the evening clear
Still bright as day, late blue-sunbright sky,
Blue above the green of the leaves with the light on them.
The branches rise and breathe and fan towards – You:
Translucent through the leaves and each vein of them,
And in my eyes as I gaze at them, whispering, stilled.

I walk back out alone behind you –
You, Lord, in the lamb on the back of the gate
With its cross like a staff where it kneels down:

ET SEQUATUR ME,
VIA EST VERITAS

Where I take the text as my own

And in a clearing just beyond the gate,
Where the long grass opens towards a field,
I found You, find You – almost tread on You
Curled there with your brown soft spikes,
Huddled up, bunched up in fear: hedgehog!
Unmoving as I stand back and laugh
Softly at myself … then as I love you,
Small person, I see it's You I'm loving
I could as easily step carelessly on …

And if I asked You for a sign You gave me that
I asked You for nothing, and You gave me my heart again

In the dark of the monastic chapel we finally go to,
Each alone — we meet and steal in at the back
Up the unlit stairs to the gallery where sit we sit apart
Gazing over the rail into the darkness —
A strange, strong energy shivers to meet me
And as I close my eyes
  — 'Brother Thomas, Brother F., and Brother Stephen are here' —
I see them come forward in a hooded trinity
Offering me a sword to draw with its gleaming hilt
Silver in the blackness as the moon slides out ...

And you talk in a whisper about your ancestors,
The Venus, and Wesley — and what it means for you
To be a bawdy poet and a believer
                                        and I believe you
As I see the South American Magdalenes dancing
With white flowers in their hair, their feet
Bare on the ground
                        under the moon that silvers down

On the swastika rock. 'Goodnight!'

Day 2

Ilkley – Malham – Gordale Scar

S unlight shimmering over my eyelids as I wake,
       Lying on my back, palms over my chest,
       Light streaming into the room, and the length of my body
Charged with clear, bright energy

                             reaching down for this pencil:

Sunlight dappling in my room
Come find me
The sunlight stronger than stone

Sunlight bathing the morning in crystal …

I see it lightening everywhere, through the walls

Dazzling bright Sun of You

                   in my inner eye

Sun that burns up every untruth
Sun, that even the eagle is a speck to

And the followers of Sheik Alla'heim you speak of, Owen,
Your warm lyrical voice echoing in my mind,
Circle it in empty white hoods …

Compassionate sun
Everything become its heart
See how all our images return there

Inner sun, and living sun

As it slants over the valley

And a voice is asking,
'Will you enter the realm of crystal?'

Sun we walk in, sun we breathe in
Heart of our eyes' light

And now

The sun in all of us! you old men chorus

The sun that flows between us in goodwill and kindness
As we talk to each other, between our eyes –

And gone blind to the sun I see it
As it streams in our receiving
Where words come, and We Are the Channel ...

As I glance up, the sunlight shadows on the wall
Two vertical planks of light to the left of the window,
The upper one swirling and the lower one still
By the vivid orange curtains ...

Sun in the Logos, and sun in the earth
Man-sun and woman-sun ...

I see her spread like a cup beneath him
                        and his incomplete circle:

Get up –
For a brisk walk, with the wind from the north now
Sweeping outside over the grass, in the light
Its blades racing in runnels like mice

And as I stand, in all that grass, gazing down in mid-step
A single yellow buttercup gleams up
Blazing yellow-gold like a sun to remind me;

And back at the Calvary, just inside the gate,
Before the Stations begin: a green strip of tree-bark
Dried out like parchment with a hole at its centre,
And to the left of it, carved in wood, EPHMO
With the light over it, and what could it mean?
A new word – ancient, but new – mysterious,
Unspoken, and untranslatable –
But the Word of God in the depth of the green

ET SEQUATUR ME ...

So brief – the stripped sheets ...

May I be with You, and You be in me
May I make the space for You to enter

And on to the forecourt where we gather to get in the bus,
'Hey, Frederica ...' in the breeze, as you embrace us,
Your eyes moist in the light, caught back

The cloud-swathed cirrus sketched wide in farewell
Over Ilkley as we leave, like a rainbow jet-trail –
And I gaze out of the window for the silence
Away from your chatter, still under the sky,
The clouds above two horses in a field on the road north

A ruin overgrown with ivy
                                          ... and it whispers,
'Bring the wind to the heart, and see what you find,'
And my heart is a cool bowl of moving sun,
My heart is this green and this road ...

We come to the grey sign for the Abbey – and surface
To walk back down the road to the Hole in the Wall
Punctured open among the thick stones where it begins:

You laugh, Gwyn, taking the step ahead of me and through
To where the steps lead down and the path curves round
With the river glinting over the grass among the sheep,
And the shell of the building, while I linger behind
Watching you walking in step ahead

And when I closen to the sky-bombed windows: the tree,
The senex tree, as dead as a tree could be
Yet alive, with its high bush of ivy and mistletoe
And fresh protruding branches – as dry and as old
As the stone, gnarled as an elephant's foot at its base,
With its bark pitted and rutted with knobbles ...
And I'm touching your balsa-dry softness in wonder
At what you've seen, white-head, guardian –
As I lay my forehead against cactus-sharp desert

And there on the grass – inexplicably –
As I walk round, stretched among the daisies
With two broken bits of stick above and below it,
A hare, its eyes closed, frozen in a leap,
Its back legs trailing and its front paws raised;
I circle it to go in at the porch:

And as I open the inner door the centuries of prayer
Echo in the chanting over the dark varnished pews
To the altar with blood-red and grey lilies
Painted on stone behind it ... Sitting then,
As you do, and finding our heads bowed – to their voices,
To the song, the deep song of the heart, resonating
In its endless soft rise-and-fall *All-e-lu-ia*
Coursing its deep passage through the blood –
The calm rising, its warmth rising in my veins ...
And in the warmth of my palms on my knees, like a fire,
As I ask

Help me listen ...

And I come back, the lilies reappearing on the stone,
Like trumpets of blood, witnesses of blood –

Consider the lilies of blood
They breathe, they stand at the height of angels

The deep light calm ... voices chatting at the back,
The taste in my mouth, the slap of donation coins,
And as I walk out through the porch, and glance up

Into the brightness, white wings flash –
And were they dove's?

The vaulted arch open to the sky, like at Tintern,
And then the river with its fast-running sunlit shallows
Running away ... as my steps quicken – Last!

Fast-forward and back into the bus, to move on:

Glimpsing the rock I call the heart's rock
Like a humped mound of green, a mountain in the shape of this
With the valley spreading either side

'the gateway to the Dales'

As we slow past a canalside, through Bill Bush
With its intimate lanes that lead us to the gateway gorge ...

To Malham, where we stop at the National Park Centre
For a walking map, and we wander looking for lunch,
Up the pavement side, the beck brown-bright in the sun
And the ducks blending with it as you smile down at them –
With the light on their backs, and the stones under them,
In the eddies of the water, and the eddies they make.

And while we sit outside the café the girl serving us
Warns us not to feed them near the road –
As two of them closen, expectantly ...
Her pet favourite got run over; and while she talks
I look at the love in her eyes,
I look at the love, her open heart, and the lightness
That doesn't say, but *is*, and *does*.

And as we walk back the sign on the Methodist Chapel
Says it all, and you stand there smiling
On the uncut grass, with its green door behind you:

> Live
> more
> lightly
> on the
> earth

That I take as a message, now we follow in line
In a loose crocodile, crossing the clapper bridge,
Because in our eyes we are all like children, thank God,
Ponderous pilgrims, and children ...

Climbing a steep stile over a drystone wall
 – and I help you over, Josephine, as tiny as a bird –
On to the Pennine Way and into a single-file meadow ...
We follow the path, at our own pace, and the land opens
Rising to the left, criss-crossed with mazy boundaries
Sketched in a pencil of low-veined Iron Age walls
Marking where the settlements and fields first were
Where the fault line runs between them

And a party of school kids closen behind us
As the stream beside us quickens, and they quicken –
Until they flood all around us with their voices
Shrill and speedy and awake ... talking names

And talking about each other – *'He's got a hamster!'*
One boy's saying as they pass us, oblivious,
And we all go towards the dog-hole in the wall
Where the sheep wait, rounded up, and the farmer waits
With his sheep-face full of death, leaning on his stick;

And they pass ahead on their journey, leaving us
Where the grass grows thick with dandelions and quietens
And the stream flow snakes slowly in among the trees
With its broad back of gleaming twilight water.
The path grows wet with its thick musk scent
Of crushed wild garlic ... Tiptoeing round its edges
As we closen to the Source and its gathering roar ...

In a clearing between the trees, into an oval pool
Surrounded by stones – it pours, falling, she pours
In two splayed streams of white, in front of our faces
As we stand and gaze ... streaming over parted thighs
With two pads of foam below in the water like breasts
– and the cool scent of salt-spray in the roar of her –
And as she roars she sings; this is her song of foam,
Her Song of Water Songs, Janet of the Foss –
Her water surrounds her like hair, white hair,
White pouring, white-headed, John, you stand watching her;

And we breathe, we breathe, we breathe out –
Wave after wave like sea, wave after wave of sea-roar
Breaks and flows through me, as you do,
Clearing my mind, all mind out, whiting it out with water.

I come to ... to where you've gone on ahead,
Leaving me with her, and I bow in thanks
And take the path up left into the sun,
Catching up with you as I breathe *wow, that was amazing!*
And you say nothing, but you seem to understand ...

And as we walk out on to the plain the Heights
Are somewhere else, too — like a green Israel —
Like the Golan Heights you sang of in the desert we're walking,
And I glance at your rucksacked back and bowed head
With your tousled hair, Tom, and the stones our feet drag on

Going into Gordale Scar … and the walls closen
As the gorge deepens, gouged out by ice —
Until they stand at cathedral height, sheer, vaulting,
And we stand with our necks craned as if looking at stars.

The rocks rise, they are the Father rocks now,
And as I stand apart it comes to me to sing
A note, a single note as if given on the air
Or given in me, a low note, low as the risen rock;
Low from the belly I sound it, and again —
And the water dividing over the rock and round it
Skirts a hole, a navel in the rock: it's a navel,
A belly-rock at the centre, like the sound
And the echo of you, Father.

And as we thread along in silence by the wall we follow
Along the Fault Line — with the gorge behind us
Where the distance opens out to Pendle Hill,
And I think of you and the witches, Alison —
I think of your roots in this sexual earth
As I see you both, pin-sized, standing there …

And your breath won't come, so David goes to fetch the bus,
Leaving us waiting (it seems for hours), and
You can't take another step, and when we sit you down
I can feel your heart beating as I'm breathing,
Your bird-heart as you sit on the grass
And we watch the lane, waiting. 'What's keeping him?'

And, fed up, you say you'll wait, Tom, as the three of us go on:

16

Crossing the lane, to the limestone pavement
Above the Cove, like a plateau –
Where the stones are broken in gaps, like an earthquake
Where the ground has cracked ... old earth has cracked
Revealing the new ... green bracken and ferns,
Where the gaps reach down, down into blackness,
And I loosen a stone with my foot between them –
Walking on to it in a dream, hardly believing
That the ground can hold, and yet it does.

You walk between them, behind us, with your stick
While you, Gwyn, you, you dance!
You dance ahead as you walk, through the breaking,
Going with the shape of each stone as you show us the way,
A woman's way, while they grow smaller, and the green rises
And how it is is how it will be, coming through.

As we glance down, two climbers hang on the rock
On the sheer side, trailing their ropes –
Descending, framed, as by a great open window ...
And as we gaze at them I'm saying, 'It's like them:
We need to come to the edge of ourselves
To go beyond the edge of the world'
                                                    and you know it,
Though how you will fly, you don't.
As we start down

You're telling me about teaching scripture to children,
And defending the right to teach it – while I warm,
I warm to your fire confronting these men
Who don't understand the Kingdom of Heaven
And who want their kids to be like they are,
Well-behaved little atheists, with no wings –
'And the children know,' you say, 'the children *know*.'

We come to a stream where a white-bellied martin
Is gliding in the light, over its water
Threading from green to green tussock as it slides between the stones

And below, in a field beneath, set among the trees
A green caravan where I dream of writing this –
Like yours, in Cornwall, where you go for solitude
To remember who you are in the silence …

The thread of it guides us down home
On through the lanes of the Dales … towards evening
When a flight of birds scatter high in the air,
Wheeling round – free-flung – unbounded,
A ram drinks out of a tree stump for a trough,
And a rider suddenly crosses the road in front of us
And disappears with his horse down an old green lane.

BELIEVE IN JESUS CHRIST AND YOU SHALL BE SAVED
The sign says at Over Kellet

And we *cross* the motorway from above …

To Carnforth, then we come to the gates:
And as we draw in through a grove of Druid trees
Towards Our Lady and its stately façade
A group of calves cross our path … and are sacred;
As one frolics, delaying us, with his brown gazing eyes
We slow in round the circle of mown wet grass.

We decide on a group session after supper …
In the long brown panelled room with its serving trolleys
We sit waiting, hungry for whatever there is –
And I notice your irritation again, silent, tight-lipped
In the brief Grace, that doesn't seem to want to shift,
And I suggest a meditation – a time and a place –
Which then gets delayed as you drift in, one by one …

And it's obvious you're angry, but not saying so,
With the burden of all the admin over you (I know!)
As we finally gather and I light a thick white candle;

And after a moment just to breathe, I ask you
To remember when you chose to come on this journey.
And what does it mean? What does being a pilgrim mean?
What is it to name yourself as that?

And when we surface in the almost dark it's like labour,
You don't want to speak – and David is silent.
Only Gwyn picks it up as she talks of broad horizons
And how the journey doesn't need to have an end;
Then there's you, Gilli, mentioning 'group expectation',
And Josephine, with 'union beyond domination',
All wise feminine words … and it gives an inch or three
And I talk about being marked from the start,
Born, as I was, on the Pilgrim's Way …

And listen, we are human, we are all here together
To closen into the heart, together – as I feel it –
And that means including *all* we are

We could pray to recognise, and we stand and join hands:
Let's be true to ourselves and our feelings
And trust that we can own them as they are
In the one presence that holds us here as Children,
And we blow out the flame … we're not One yet!

And upstairs as we go for tea the anger stays
Strangely as maybe it was meant to do –
Trust your feelings, your tears in the fence, your fire
As we meet this unctuous priest, a visiting patriarch
Hiding behind his Orthodox beard and glasses,
Rationalising *not* giving intercommunion –
And my hackles rise

Because this sacrament is for everyone, I say to you
In the Name of Love we have forgotten.
Or, Father, what are you? A slick professional
Wriggling on the sofa and talking about the tennis
And God knows what other trivia: but not the one thing;
The one wholly essential thing we have to come back to
That can bring us all together … and Theology?
You don't need a university to do *that*.

Ah, is it Love or Fear? I think it's fear –
But let it be love. As I kiss you both goodnight,
I kiss you though I barely know your names.

Day 3

'1652 Country' – Briggflatts

R ain, waking ... the grey air come down,
Wrapping the air around in leaden slate-soft sleep,
Whispering as my hand moves across the page:

The fire burns to ash, and the ash breaks to tears
So it rained in the night, and the morning is grey;
The trees stand listening, their leaves moving,
The trees stand with the rain dripping off them,
The trees stand in the wisdom of tears
That sink to their roots, none of them wasted
As they gather sap from them, and the tears are pearls;
Each tear drop is silver in the eyes of the moon,
And if you cry your eyes will shine too,
They will gather their lustre and be beautiful;
So let your tears fall under your feet,
Let your tears feed your soul through the soles of your feet.

Pilgrim you are here to feel ... this voice is saying;
You are here to feel where the heart has been valid.

I watch the rain dripping down over the slates outside the window,
Seeming to sink into the slate as it slides ...
And a drain outside draws the water to its centre:
It's the *other* sun now, the Sun of Water,
The inner sun that draws us to the centre

Waiting, and David takes the van to pick up Eva
(Our guide for the day) as we loosely gather –
Sitting around scanning the books: waiting interminably.
As the minutes pass into an hour, all it does is rain
As you pace between phone calls, ready to snap ...

Rain, breaking you down too
And still you can't seem to let go –

Until it arrives, in its own time.
We finally leave for Levenshall, leavened by the rain
 – you drive, vaguely concerned, in tense silence –
Passing hay bales, with the hay like shed hair
And the cloud down over the hill to the right
As the land on the other side moves towards mountain

And the plan dissolves. That's how it is;
The river plan dissolves over Levens Bridge
 – with its island of weed the water skirts round –
To walk into Kendal, along it …
And as we sit in the pub no one can decide what to do.

Muted reaction. Blame. Adolescent depression.
Until you come up with a better idea –
'I'll take you to 1652 Country', and at last we're agreed

And with Eva in the front seat the rain has softened in,
Something has softened, something has given
The way the rain breathes, and we surrender
As it glistens over the road and under the tyres
Hissing, or whispering, and beads the side windows …

And, relenting, you talk about George Fox
Until I'm lost in the story, seeing him as you speak
Standing on top of Pendle Hill in the light
Like a soft golden glow around him, where the cirrus clouds
Were thousands coming to meet him, three thousand
Waiting for him on Firbank Fell.

You smile, but more than smiling
You talk with the light in your eyes, the light
That doesn't need to smile because it is what it is …

And we wait in the silence after your words.

The road, a long border of mist and rain
Winding round a lane off it into the Lune Valley,
Moon Valley, in the softness, with trees I'm remembering
– like a déjà vu, they seem so familiar –
As we climb its steep side through shorn green hedges.

'Tell us another one, Tom' – and you do,
Having asked us if we know the story about Penn:
A friend of his comes to him holding his gun
And he looks at him in silence (as you may imagine)
Then says quietly, with his eyes down,
'William, wear thy sword for as long as thou canst'

And the Indian chief adds,
'I look to hear where the words come from,'
And their purity stills the air as we breathe it …
As I think of them, founding fathers, true fathers,
And *Pennsylvania*, if we could see it –

And we closen to the fell, up a narrow wet lane
Where the rain is streaming and the sky is white,
Cloud-mist white over the contours and the rock
Scoured and scratched bare out of the grassy hillside:
Rain, and wind – and as we come round the fence we see
Its blue plaque and white writing:

LET YOUR LIVES SPEAK

I stand up where you preached,
The wind and rain driving on my face,
The energy under my feet like a voltage –
And I can feel you alive in the whole air
With the cloud beneath in the field like people,
Your people – a multitude – gathered;

23

I can feel the words as they come to your lips,
Given, like the wind; as it breathes in my mouth
I can feel how You speak, and make us Your Own

Then it's enough ...
                    and I climb down drenched
Where the pine trees stand with their branches blown back
And you hurry to the van, an anorak over your head –

And we drive down to Briggflatts, seeing nothing for rain,
Only a grey identical bridge we're crossing the other way
– with its vista of trees, past shoal banks ...

Then we park, awkwardly reversing in the narrow lane,
And walk along to the Friends' Meeting House
With its cottage garden, and open porch-way
Under a narrow leaded window and the house date that reads
'Anno Do.', then a star, and beneath, '1675' –
As you bare your Quaker heads, and I bow mine
Inside into the musty air and varnished depth ...

But 'musty' isn't right; it's the smell of stillness –
Of centuries of listening absorbed into the wood,
And though it's like a schoolroom, nothing is taught here,
Only the humility to listen in the silence, the presence,
And if the silence wants to speak, to speak ...
Standing, we stand silently, for a moment, gazing up
At the beams above the little stairs to the gallery;
And as you talk I wander up to the back where I find
A copy of *To the Flock about Sedburgh.*

   'Everyone in your measure wait upon God ...'

Something strangely warms and quickens
With the clarity of rain behind my eyes
As I start to copy the paragraph down

'And mind that which is pure in one another …'

One word echoing, 'pure', 'the pure'
— like a white feather, floating, falling —
In all the sonorous rich beauty of the words,
One uncapitalised word the whole text is pointing to,
That whites out the rest, that makes it transparent
To the light and the gold infused in every syllable,
Stress, nuance, and ancient timeless turn of phrase —

'And none of you be sayers (only) but doers of the Word …'

And the promise: *'it will lead you out of the world'*,
Out of the world, and out in it, and into the earth
That is the Kingdom within, that can see and touch it,
And see and feel it as it is, as Eden …

And I come down to find you've found
A copy of Bunting's *Briggflatts*, and as you peruse it
The old king at Keats House floods back to mind
And I lean over your shoulder: 'Yes, he's buried here.'
You tell me where the cemetery is, just up the lane,
And I realise I'd forgotten you'd died, five years ago,
In all that newfound summer love-light blazing in me.

I wander up the lane, quietly alone,
Remembering you, and your slowworm's song,
Your strong Northumbrian tone and unhesitating sound,
But most of all your warmth, in that one handshake,
And the brightening glimmer in your quickening eyes …

I reach the little green gate, among the yews,
And among the anonymous headstones I find yours
Simply cast, like them, unadorned — only your name
And beneath it the dates

1900–1985

With the sun-bleached grass reaching my feet,
The length of you –

I thank you for all you hammered and gave
Out of the forge of yourself – may I do the same –
And as I do I feel a warmth under my feet
In the sodden after-rain wet cold grass,
I feel a warmth, I seem to see you lying there
In the Summerland, there, under the earth
In sunlight, under the blond wet grass as I speak,
And you say *feel the ground* – and I can

Thank you, old father; and as I touch it
I rub it on my belly under my shirt, heart, brow;
A palmful of your flesh soaked up into the grass
Warm on my hands as breath …

And then we're leaving for Goose Green …

                                 lost on the way

In a myriad of lanes that all look the same –
They all seem to lead where there's no sign
But the green of the trees and the name

Until we find your green porch with its white door
And plain flagged patio, where you welcome us in
With your bread skirt and fried-eggs smile, Marlene
And John, with his loose trousers, and the smell of the dog –
A mongrel that nobody wanted, but you …
With your love of music and yearning for poetry.

We sit and talk about George Fox and Wesley,
Rival Quakers (here) – and sheer narrow-mindedness
When you regale us with the local cemetery fiasco
Where they're fighting for plots against a car park,

A bloody car park, for God's sake, as it all contracts;
I see we're in a tunnel of human wrangling,
A contracted universe where all that matters
Is you get six feet or less to be buried in
When you're as good as dead anyway ... and we tunnel on.

You talk about the long root of imperialism
Weighed in the balance with the Berlin Wall
And I talk about how it's creativity or violence
And you say, 'It must be wonderful being young,'
And yet it's for all of us now, and no escaping
When you tell us about the darkness at Dudley nearby
Where a dominating husband and arthritic wife
Have a deaf and blind boy who wants a *camwa*
But she says, 'Don't tell Dennis!' and what can you do?

You pray – we pray – we wait for it to break;
You follow your fire into the heart of the pain ...

The van arrives, and we go in for the meeting,
Three miles, and through the wet streets of Kendal
Where the Meeting House stands back down cobbles
And the door is open where you've already arrived:

Inside, past a wall of notices, the plain open room
With its plain wooden chairs, like a silent tea party,
Where we come in and sit, waiting to begin ...
I glance round at your faces, white witness faces,
Not of this time, yet of it, and connected
By the same look in your eyes that's as soft
And that even under the strip lighting is stronger
Than the sun would be, shining in through the windows ...

As we settle to silence and the presence
That shadows the air in lightness all around,

That breathes as we do, without a body,
Filling the room over our heads …

Until finally it speaks when you break it like a wafer,
Clearing your throat as you begin to talk about water
And water in its simplicity, before the Gospel –
How when you were in Africa it was the simple things,
Like bringing irrigation, that really spoke of Love;
How the Africans knew it in their patient wisdom
(they knew the difference between preaching and action).

And in the silence that follows, a man in a white shirt
With a tense serious face and tightly folded tie,
I pray

In the name of the rose, let the water also be wine

And you smile, Gwyn
                            and as you drop us off back
It's the wine that's with me. We decide on a walk
Now the sky's clear and dry, and the night inviting;
And as we start up the lane I laugh with you and say,
'We are the night pilgrims –
we only journey under the moon!'

We reach the end: then which way? You guess right,
And we follow to where we cross above the motorway,
Teeming beneath us – making the vertical –
And as we leave its roar behind us in the deepening light
The air begins to quieten, we come back to breathing,

And by the laneside you pause by an orange blossom,
Inhaling it as you bow to its scent
Of sweet dry powder and dew – as I do …
Suddenly it comes to me to say, as we walk on,
'There's a song in us that's always there,'

And I can feel it here, rising and closening
Until it's the closest thing there is to us now:
'Don't you think the song in us is always there?'

As you glance down a frog on your path
Is crossing by the grassy edge ...
It's a gift, and then there are nothing but gifts!
I'm thinking, or saying, then you say it,
You write the line as you glance back briefly behind you
Into the light deepening over the wide hills:
'I don't know if that's the last light, or the first,'
The first beginning light, the beginning ...
And I touch your arm, smiling: '*That's* the poem.'

As we walk on, honeysuckle wafts on the air
Lining the hedge-top, drifting towards us
And I breathe it in with the after-rain;
I falter to speak, and you say it so calmly – '*Ecstasy*' –
Picking some –

And as we closen up towards a gate by a field
I think of our communion, finding myself saying,
'Maybe we need an altar for it.'
'Or a tree,' you reply
And suddenly it's there, over to the right
In near silhouette, just beyond the gate we climb.
We walk over the tussocks, between the thistles, to it:
A hawthorn with its red berries glowing ...

You put it there, you place the honeysuckle there,
Then you dance, you're dancing round the tree for joy –
Three times, for joy, for the child in our hearts,
And I follow you; and in a moment it's done.

As we start back down you pause to ask me,
'Do you ever feel you don't belong here?'

We gaze down at the outline of the hills below us
In the grey, elongated air – and I'm saying,
'We're guests here – and, well, the wind has blown us here
And we have far to go,' and you nod, quietly,
'And sometimes it seems impossible …', the earth
Dense and covered as if completely in mist,
But what we bring is a seedling, and we can feel it
In our hearts as the thread of threads
Even though it stretches beyond all I can see –
And I add, 'We need so much patience.'

And as we walk on I talk about Christ and Mary
In what they made together that is the mystery
For what a man and a woman can be now,
And a bat flits and circles our heads.
There's the man in me who is really me,
And the woman in you behind the woman who laughs,
She knows … then you make me laugh too!

You tell me the parable about the bell rope, which ends
If you feel yourself going up, let go!
                                        – and we do.

Day 4

The Lakes and Airey Force Valley

And as I wake, stiff, on the camp bed
  – in John's electronics room … with the light
Filtering through the dun brown curtains behind –
Two key words come: 'the inner man' and 'expanse'.

I sleep, and the night becomes dreaming
 – half-awake I sit up remembering –
I sleep, and let it all sink to the level of dreaming
Where it becomes the dream I will dream I am dreaming,
Dreaming-awake, dreaming-knowing … as we walk
That *the earth is free in each moment*, for each of us.

I glimpse where we were, out the back
Where the curve of the hill rises with the fields,
Its trees concealing the thread of the lane where we were …
As we sit in silence at the breakfast table
Where the lights are too bright and the food's way too much!
'You sleep?' 'God, yes' – a gesture is enough.

Sunday, hymn-day – and the minibus comes
Leaving the hymn you wrote unplayed, unsung,
Leaving you with the light of it in your smile
As you stand for a brief snap, the dog round your legs
As you hold him still four inches above his head …
And we go back in to the meeting in Kendal.

Sunlight now, invisible through the windows
And inner sun, as we centre down, in the downflow
Building around the crown of our heads …
Breathing into our hearts as it whispers in silence …
You talk about this element in all religions

That is quietness, 'not claiming to know the whole truth',
And, standing, you describe your stained-glass lantern
With its candle in the middle you've been shown
Where the glass *is all the faiths lit from within*
And as you speak (glancing at your hand)
I can almost see it, as you can

While you add how we can 'better feel other faiths'
Having been outside *all* of them, even exiled from them;
And you quote this in your clear-voiced emptiness:

Lord of all being, I give you my all
If e'er I disown you, I stumble and fall
But sworn in glad service Your Word to obey
I walk in Your Freedom to the end of the day ...

Hearing it as I never have ... as it hangs
And I watch your bowed heads
I wonder, have you all been alive since then?
It's as if you've all been in some special realm of soul
You've reappeared from, on this same bare floor
With its plain table, Bibles, and roses ...

When I turn to you, Beatrice, with your bird-bright eyes
You tell me about the little the early seekers possessed:
'They were following Spirit where it took them,
Believing only that there's a way of love
That will show us *its* way inside us as it enters.
And to have that idea is so important; it changes us.
Each one of us can touch that quality of life
We see in one another' — and I see in your eyes
What you mean in every fibre of your being.
No one could be more alive, more agelessly alive,
And when you smile, and your smile holds, it sends
A shivering into my chest as I breathe,
As if I've always known you —

And now I wait outside to say goodbye.
I will walk in Your Freedom.

The land rising to meet the light, the whole land
                                    as we enter the Lakes

Glancing out, the cloud light moving up the mountain,
Sunlight over the green of it underneath, rising
                                    up Helvellyn and Scafell Pike

Then down over Great Calva with its deep breadth of water
As the road winds and the bus slows ...
The whole land breathing up
Now we pause for a moment beside a length of low railing

Then I take us down and we look out for a pub,
Finding *The Mortal Man.* You laugh, John,
In your octogenarian glee. 'That's me!' you say,
That's grounding for all our immortality,
Our fading empty stomachs ... and I need a drink;
And as we sit surrounded by landscapes and old sepia prints,
Talking about the meeting, and 'centring down',
You remark about the challenge of going at a snail's pace
That is the soul's pace (I say) or mortal pace (if you prefer)
And the joke is we're talking about the same thing ...

We leave to continue ... the view down is Brotherswater,
Over the low wall with its rock-island like a steamer
And the light on the other side merging with the cloud

As we follow a stream by the road, at walking pace,
And the ripples on the lake and the cloud's moving,
And even in the quickening song of the water,
Everything is at walking pace, everything at breathing pace,
Everything at dreaming pace when we remember to be

We closen to Airey Force Valley, reverse in to park,
And as we walk down, *it* comes ...
It comes with the gentle breath of the woods,
With the stream echoing, spread like a dove's breast over me:
Airey Force Valley, and the strength of the breath,
Whispering among the branches, that is gentleness,
Where you walked, William Wordsworth, with your inspiration gone
And it breathed to you, it quickened in your heart again,
Your heart breathed and softened ... it came
And it's still here, haunting the air.

We go down to the Source, the Falls,
Down the steep steps where it rushes like a white scarf
Of foam and spray, trailing between the branches;
We descend to the Source now, among the crowd
Drinking it in through their cameras, walling it off
As its roar blasts down clefting the rocks
Under a half-moon bridge among bracken and ferns,
Plunging, plummeting, pulsating, pure –
And as I stand there a single green leaf,
A perfect green-veined beech leaf,
Falls, drifts into the centre of the stream
With its white foam scur
And God-sized stones scattered around,
And I turn

And after elbowing gently through the daze
And walking a little way among the trees
I go up to the bridge ... where we queue
To lean over

And suddenly I see the beauty *of what it is to fall*
As the two streams of water, dividing, come together
Shattering in breaking moving ice
As I lean out –
To plummet, to plunge, to dance down,

To plunge, to fall, face down,
To float as soft as spray-white feathers,
Spray-white floating feathers,
Oh the beauty of what it is to let go
And fall like the moment for ever –

And as we wander back up through the woods again
To the rough layby at the top, where you're waiting
 – reading in the bus, hungry for some space –
I'm needing to be alone, too, needing to be silent,
So you suggest we walk the other way ...
Thirsting for the height beyond this crowded deepening,
I set off up the path across the lane, while you linger

And then break free through the bracken and long grass
Up the steep side to the right, towards the rim
That's a ridge of trees beyond the sheep, above the lake.
I climb breath for breath and step for step,
Swallowing the air and the taste in my mouth,
Past a fallen dead elm with its branches like antlers;
And the wind, the lake below, and the hill mountains
Like a bowl, a broth of air, as it blows ...

This dead tree with its bark-stripped branches
Is the dead tree of my past, 'a lesson learnt',
A dead tree of words: but beside it, a living one
And God alone walks on these mountains under the cloud
With his Son like a speck somewhere inside him ...

Before I go, I turn up to the living tree,
Placing this black-lined journal at its feet
Where the hollow in the grass is shaped like a head,
For my head, and I kneel and bow my forehead into it;
And the tree is speaking to me, then
Is saying, 'Think with me ... think with earth,'
As I breathe and say

Let my mind be a servant and no longer a master

And, coming to, I leave my mind there
– I leave my words, I leave my books –
For You.

As I walk back down, it's raining,
I side-step on the grass and then stride,
And all I know is *the living height was climbed*
And, as I think it, the sun glows out for a moment,
Gold on my face, outlining my shadow,
Deep green behind me on the hill's side.

Bending to drink the rain-sweet water from the stream
With its taste of rock, I lift it into my palms
With the rain still falling into it;
Rainwater, sweet rock,
Sun-stream, quenching my dead nicotine thirst

And as we drive on
                    the cloud, the cloud pouring down in light!

Down the road ahead, in the distance, under its low thick curtain,
The cloud breaking in white, raying down light, raining light –
As we closen
            and take the Mosedale turning

Leaving its promise there
                    as the sky darkens
Grainy over the hillsides and the dotted farmhouses
And we drive in silence under its spell
And come to the house under Carrock Fell;

A mound of grey shale looming over it,
Once a Roman hill fort up the stony sheer side

Pocked with outcrops of furze and whatever can grow
Or cling with its roots under the thin surface soil.

It lowers like a shadow, a high-voltage pylon,
When we get out and glance round its Georgian façade ...
Then we head for rest into our separate rooms.

I come with you, and while you read my white poem book
I'm sitting cross-legged on the bed, breathing in,
Closing my eyes, plunged into stillness-silence –
And it's not sleep I want or mean, but listening
As you turn the pages and sip at your tea ...

And then you say, 'It's like a mountain.'
The flow of its shape is like a spiral mountain.
You sketch its ascending curve with your hand –
And I remember you, Valentinus, recalling what you say
About our names being called in the mist as we climb,
Unable to see each other, only hearing that voice calling

'John', 'Gwyn', 'Carole' ... its ghostly cries
Like a song unsung, each single note fading ...
Then I'm asking, what is it that strips away
The layers of what we are to reveal our centre?
What else is it but the unknown, the unnamed
That has secretly always been living us, as us –

As I hear myself in the mist, and you sit with the book
Still open at the end of the bed, on your knee,
I ask you what the difference is between the teacher
And the pilgrim – 'And isn't it this?' –
You don't need to disagree ...

But they don't seem to like us here: it's weird,
None of us knows what we've supposed to have done wrong,
Their eyes like slate as they serve us

While we sit at three tables discussing agendas ...
They said, 'Vegetarians are very welcome.'
'What do you reckon, then?' Tom: 'No idea' –
And I wonder if it's the fell they live under ...

So many questions, and it's so easy to judge
The face or fate that conceals its suffering
Who knows ... but as we walk the rainy wet road
The blasting squall propels us under the hawthorn hedge
For cover that we share with the cattle nosing ...
As we wait for it to lighten;

Then we walk over the old bridge-way's
Brief detour of green before we rejoin the tarmac,
To a derelict building at the corner with two horses
Tethered and feeding, as if abandoned ...
And turn back in the cold as the rain again begins,
Then abruptly clears and lifts

Leaving the air good to breathe and the road to walk on,
Before it begins all over again – the whole air unsteady –
As I gaze ahead reading the language of the clouds,
The grey like an underplate, trying to shift ...
The light cloud above it, the cloud trying to move
As we're blown, pushed back by the wind –

Then rose, ahead, barely; but a streak of rose northwards

And in this house under the fell,
Under its looming pile of shale,
Mosedale spelt Misery Dale,
Pray

Lighten all those living in grey
Whose eyes are still cold when they smile.

Day 5

Back o' Skidda – Carlisle

The wind in the morning, buffeting the eaves,
And outside, through the window's squares,
The sun sliding in shadow over the green of the fell,
My thoughts … and the painful laughter of the hens.

We decide on a walk – 'Back o' Skidda' – the three of us
While we've still got a morning, before we have to move on.
You gaze at a map, tracing its brown-veined contours,
You've already half planned it, and you're already dressed.
'Are you coming, then?' 'No,' No thanks,' which leaves us –
David with his rolled up socks and stick, ready,
And you, Gwyn, with your Everest blue anorak … in complicity,
Because we all want to do some real wild walking.

The wind outside greets us, with fast-moving cloud …
The rain's still holding off – so far, so good –
And maybe the sky will be clear … or maybe it won't,
What chance? The first cold drops are already starting,
And there's no turning back from the breath, or this,
There's no turning back when you've said, 'I breathe.'

Reaching the long path turning off the road to the right –
'This must be where we go' – you check the map
And I wonder at your rolled-up sleeves and bare head,
But you're still smiling and your eyes are bright.
You pull up your hood. And immediately the path is wind
Sweeping up the whole length of the valley it funnels –
Shrouding us in silence as we bow forward to the path's gradient,
Its steepening grey shale and slate gleaming with rain,
As we tread, step by step, under our feet
Step by step, and stone by stone, as I breathe –

Hands behind my back, the ground coming up to meet me.

Stone by stone until I've long lost count,
The rain thickens, and we haven't spoken for a mile.
What is this? Purgatory? Pure driving grey –
Finally we turn to shield ourselves from its needles,
Turning our backs, exhausted, and crouching as if to shit.
Will it ever end? Remember what you said, Gwyn!
Till finally we go on ... until the stream bisects us –
Then the path runs out, leaving us in grass wilderness
And you're trying to hold on to the flimsy torn map
The wind is ruthlessly tattering ...

We branch up left, up the grass to the hill's edge:
Then we glimpse the tarn, slate-grey as thundercloud,
As we closen ... all this rock become water –
All this rock become rainwater, like its colour ...
We stand on the edge of its freezing bleak shore,
The rain plashing on its surface like beads of glass
Half white, driven in wavelets, dissolving, bubbling,
Liquid over a mirror there is no reflecting

And you turn to the crags to go for the top.
Sheer rock, the rock grass, with its lichen and ferns
And I turn and glance, the wind-blown rain
Driving over the skein of the water like steam.
As I go back to my hands and feet to each slippery hold,
We pass the edgy sheep saying, 'You must be crazy!'
They shift to one side, unable to run,
The wind rises and loudens, bearing down,
And as I crawl on the Belly of the Mother I think of you
As if I was with you, with each fern in front of my face.
At least you got my postcard! 'The message is earth.'
The message is you as it always was ...
Guiding me to fall in love with the ground
But not fall here, or fall asleep as I could ...

And then suddenly as we reach the top the wind is treble
And the rain is horizontal – where are you?
We are stopped in our tracks, each of us –
Brought to a standstill where we are standing ...
And in the cloud, cloud-white mist coming over like a veil
I can't see – I can't shout – it doesn't mean anything –
You disappear ahead somewhere over the brow,
Leaving us in whiteness – roaring whiteness – whiteness
Blitzing our senses, all at once, as we struggle to stand
Until all we are is like hurtled raindrops, images,
On a screen of interference, snow-blind with static;
All there is is the whiteness pouring through – *where are you?*

'Where's David, for God's sake?' I'm roaring
As you shake your hooded head and open your hands –
And we huddle down to the edge out of the blast, waiting.
'He must be going down the other way.' 'Well, I hope so.'
Gone over the brow into the whiteness
 – and it's as if he has –
Gone beyond all words and images, all telling,
Gone into the roaring breath of God, speechless to 'I am'.
And there's no sleeping on this edge where we crouch.
'We better get down while there's still time.'
And it's true, you could die up here. Why not?
So you inch ahead, cold on your heels, to the bone,
And I follow you, catching at green grass, hanging on

I straighten up and side-step, and slip once
While I'm thinking *stop thinking* as we go down,
Leaving the whiteness behind us with its eerie glow –
For the whiteness ahead, where the rain cloud hangs
Pouring sheer over the grass and the scattered sheep
And the fields below ... where we glimpse you – 'There he is!' –
Coming down the other way, as you guessed,
And smiling as if nothing unusual has happened, the madman,
The sane man ... or not quite smiling, because something had,

And that is in a privacy we will never know
This side of the Light, and of our faces ...
'Thank God you're OK! What happened?' And you beam
You are more than OK, much more. You are alive

As we come down to walk with the stream, relieved –
Relieved to be descending, able to walk upright,
We step down towards the Round House bridge
There, in a clearing of trees ... We arrive
At its thin wooden length, its gate flapping open,
Which we leave open, with the Country behind us,
As we walk slowly down the lane
With space between us, as we need, to be alone ...
Passing the black-faced sheep and the two patchwork fields
Brown and light and dark brown, to where we began.

Leaving now ... north towards Carlisle; I drive us
Out of the Lakes, thinking of Merton ... as you talk behind me,
And then the small needs we have reassert themselves
Because we're creatures of them: needing stamps, needing to pee.
We stop at Caldbeal, where the Priest's Café is closed,
You go into the wool shop with its sheepskins and kitsch,
And I look around to find a place to have a leak,
Sneak down beside the other one behind a bush,
And the woman sees me and she don't like it at all!

We sit in awkward silence, ringed by awful pictures.
Even the scones are rotten ... We pay up and go,
Breathing out, relieved
                        north again, you map reading,
The fells gone behind us and the land flattening ...

The road slowly rises to the hill's brow, and
There it is, suddenly ahead
                        the plain of Scotland!
Spreading in the sunlight beyond the clouds as we gaze

Over Border Country at its green fields and horizon, like a dream.
As the road begins to dip down again, I see it:
First we see the vision, then we have to walk to it
First we see the height, then it's the valley's depth
Detail by detail of the road — that is the journey ...

We settle back to laughter, chatter, and silence,
You track the pub names, John, hoping for The Immortal Man,
But there are only kings and queens and princes, none of us
Let alone the *New* Man — but give us bright names;
Come on, let's make some up. What's yours, Gwyn? Tom?
— and no, Mr Linton, this ain't a pub crawl.
What's mine? The Rampant Feminist will do nicely,
Neat tequila on the rocks, holy water on ice,
Bloody Magdalenes and beautiful conversation.

We pass a sign to Rose Castle (of the Heart), left
As we go right ... slowing behind a hayrick trailer
With its grass and blond straw hanging, hair of the earth,
The first of the summer grass ... and all my memories of summer
In this grey No-Summer, this Zero Summer —
Of grey transforming into blue, grey then blue
The colour of now, the colour of the future.

We come to the outskirts ... with its boxes for homes,
Pass a huge brick chimney on Junction Street,
Vaulting, sheer, vertical — brick by brick, like Babel —
And then the old red of the city walls we enter,
Looking for the car park the other side of the cathedral ...

We climb up the Sally Port steps, through the West Wall,
And then walk the to the Market Square with its precinct
By Carel Cross where we decide to meet at the service.

Suddenly, people and crowds ... as I retrace my steps
And you half stand at a loss, unsure what to do,

Then I'm a stranger alone in the Great Border City
Torn in its tug of war through eight centuries
Vanishing into the mists of the drizzling rain ...
Into traffic as I wait to cross this busy main road –

And the Castle on its low mound of grass
Is a shell – a nothing – a scoured red sandstone heart,
Only the air palls like granite as I pass through the arch,
Its misery imprinted, metallic and immovable as cannon.
And if you go down into the dungeon with its filthy metal frames,
And damp swept floor, no one lingers, no one stays,
There's nothing to see or feel, only darkness, pain –
The darkness of a dead heart where nothing can change.

The slit view on to the grass, up the steps, says it all:
That's all you can see of life or living ...
And even in De Ireby's Tower
The rest is frozen, gone by like a reconstructed dream,
Gone by in coloured panels, history gone past –
Only the prisoner's art remains (and that's justice)
Carved into tiny red squares in the stone –
And I bend to find the faces of Sheela na Gig
Triumphant, mermaid, tortured and untamed
And that's what they dreamt of, and all they had to dream ...

I walk down by the cathedral, and stand
Where the east window rises in reversed-out splendour
With the light on the grass like slate, sun on slate,
Up into the filigree framing of its vault.
I glance down on the grass, and there, woven in saxifrage
And sown into the soil in outline, is a boy
A green boy, a blind boy reaching out his hand
As I gaze into the blossoming of his eyes
And to a dream that is born out of a living earth
That can see like that ...
                              and I take it

And, walking inside early, I meet the verger
Walking the other way in his black cassock
I get the feeling he's just pulled on over his clothes
Without much conviction. I meet his eyes: he's glad to talk
And hustles me into the presbytery offering tea,
Sweeping aside my vague surprise with 'Of course'
As he fiddles around to find sugar and spoons.
'Do you know what "verger" means, eh?' – a wink in his eye –
'It's the Latin for "penis", one who clears space in a crowd.'
I smile, and he gestures waving with his hand
Among the imaginary hoi polloi

As I glance up behind him at a gaggle of vergers
In a black and white photo, a gaggle of penises –
And he points out the Archbishop: 'That's the boss, of course.'
When I tell him where we're going, he mentions one
'Watson, ah yes, he died there leading a pilgrimage.'
He died where? On Iona. Yes, but where?
And you don't have to tell me –
He died on Dun I, on the mountain. I can see him
As you talk on and all your gossip goes silent.
He died on the mountain, that's what you came to tell me.

I thank him for the tea. ('Of course, I better get on now.')
I wander out into the nave as the bells start to chime,
Gazing at the vaulted ceiling with its blue and gold stars
Above the choir, encrusted among shields, crowns and roses
'To build the city of Dioce whose terraces are the colours of stars.'
Old Ezra, your Canto comes back to mind –
Although it wasn't here you were dreaming, and nor am I
And I wouldn't call it Dioce, but Jerusalem
Wherever that is, in Albion, in the streets of our hearts …
As the bells sleepily surround the time
With their after-echo like a brass harpsichord,
And when time goes to sleep we shall find it,
When time learns to dream we will begin it

We will *begin it now* … as you begin to arrive.

And we sit for the service as if it's arranged for us.
There's no one else here – in the regal wooden seats
Carved elbow to elbow and arm to arm at the sides …
The boss (the Canon) stands and gives the proclamation
Like a seasoned performer, and I listen for his tone,
His deep voice urbane as we come on to sinning

'We are truly sorry …'

And it seems he is, as I glance at you …
Then he hurries through the psalm, 'Come bless the Lord,'
'May the Lord bless you from Zion,' wherever that is,
Before we come to the Magnificat and the Nunc Dimittis
Where his voice can't help deepening at the beauty
And I pray the poem with him, because I know it's real,
As you do, your eyes briefly closed beside me:
And still all I can glory in is the name of the Holy Spirit,
For Your Breath we cannot legislate, only love.

And we come to the Apostles' Creed; this is it:
What do I believe? What can I truly say?
Only what I feel as an answering echo, a quickening
Like a slow warmth or fire in my blood
And it's not the Father only, but the Mother almighty,
It's not the judgement, but wordless understanding,
Not the holy catholic church, but all churches,
All temples, all faiths, all living bodies in You
In Your Name that is the name of resurrection,
And the body – yes, *the body* – the body at last

But then it rises, at last, in the light of the last prayer
As the choir's voices ascend in the background, rehearsing
Where the words are leaven, because they're yours
As you give them like an improvisation:

'Bring us together, Lord,
That the broken body of Your Son
We lay before this broken world may be healed.'

And the spell breaks; your head bows, and the doors are open.

We crowd into an Indian after picking up Margot
(Tennyson – the named transposed into Yiddish).
You sit beside me, Dorothy, your frozen shoulder
Making me think of our invisible wounds, our crosses ...
The restaurant buzzes round us with its music and orders
As we swell to toast and take in more of our company
Like a First Supper with real food and red wine.
'And the last shall be first' – how's that? You laugh

And as I look around our candlelit faces to the walls,
At Shiva and Shakti, and Krishna in his gay open colours,
You explain how Hindu images are a way of education
(As you meet my eyes, Margot) 'for going beyond'.
You tell me with your accent as rich as thick incense
About the series of temples in sequence you saw
Which led to a temple that has nothing, an emptiness gate:
Emptiness – space – *void*, and I breathe

And beneath the Church of the Holy Sepulchre, Jerusalem,
'If you can persuade the priest to let you have the key
You can go down step after step into the ground ...
Down to the three-thousand-year-old foundations ...'
There I descend
                              and the restaurant briefly disappears.
I go down, as if under my feet, under the table;
Down to the level where it really happened –
Down for the living, still living water,
'Down into yourself', and your belly, Magdalene,
Down into the midnight sun of gold –

Now we walk back to the B&B. I call you in a corner,
South, all the way down the line, to update you
And if we can let go of the form, the name of the thing we want,
It can enter your life, it can enter you as 'you'.

And north over the suburb building the island waits
Where the light lingers under the dark breadth of clouds;
Over the houses and the neon streetlights' reflections
Beyond the TV screen with its ephemera

The island waits that the one light rays down on,
Under the sun, from the Sun of suns that has no name.

Day 6

Crossing the border – Langholm – Samye Ling

W aking in grey, to the blank screen ... we eat,
Then the sun breaking through as the cloud clears outside
And shining on the blue of the minibus as we board to get on
our way
Back through the city
                    and pausing: the blue
Hovering above the cathedral and up the east window
Above the castle with its solitary white and red square flag
And down Paternoster Row ... its cobblestones in shadow
Reaching through an arch on to the lit wall of a passageway
Past an old-fashioned lamp post
                    where a bird hovers,
Its wings a blur between the shadow and light of the buildings –
Silhouetted, as the shutter blinks, against the blue of the sky

I bring down the camera –
And it's only this moment, these moments, so fleeting,
You have to catch on the wing, to snatch at like koans, and be
Snatched, snapped in, in the picture – to see
Life quickening at all its silently written edges that say *Alive*,
Here, now, always, and never
                    as the hand slows,
Its palm meeting air and dissolving ...

Pure breath of blue, outbreath of blue
                    and as we drive,
The land rising again, we glimpse Scotland, towards the border
And we decide we'll walk the last mile to cross it on foot –

And now we closen ('Check the map ...') to where the bridge *is it*,
Above the treetops, as the road curves round into fields.

I switch the engine off as we glide in sunbright silence, excited,
At the beginning of the downhill dip, where we pull in
To a grass verge – 'I'll come back and get it.' 'OK,' you say
'Everyone out!' 'Come on, you idle pilgrims!'

And as we walk in file down the centre white lines
With no traffic in sight, listening out behind,
I turn and glance back to see you raise your arms, Gwyn,
Up above your head with your palms and fingers open.

And as we closen, my heart's pounding
Before the gesture some part of me is making
That I can't explain – I only know I have to kneel,
Really kneel now, asking
                                        and I do, quietly
With you all around me … and no matter
Nothing could be more natural: your silence tells me.
I'm just about halfway over the bridge
With my palms flat on the tarmac, when I ask You

May I be with You, may I let You in
And may I stand as I am in my full height

And as I do, You grant it, You grant it in blood
Silently, in no language but the heart's.
I feel it rising up into me, and through,
And without even realising it I'm up on my feet and over

And where a narrow path leads down, over a stile among nettles,
Past the bridge, down to the river under it,
I follow where you've gone
                                        down where its reflection
Is a rainbow of stone in the gleaming brown sunlit water;
I straddle a rock on the bank, feet dangling,
Wild flowers beside me: dandelion, clover, colt's foot,
Purple vetch … and the colours of the flowers in the grass

And the shape of the stone spell *wholeness*
Above and below ... wholeness, and gateway
Like the mouth of a womb, into a Greater Life ...

And as I stand, the sun's blaze reflecting in the water
Is a disc in its liquid like silk, silk and oil,
Where the stones under it and the dark of the water are like cloud
And the sun is a moon too, a blazing pearl –
And in between my eyes when I close them there's only light,
In the sun between the bridge and its reflection

While the water drifts, eddies, and ripples
Between the banks downstream in slicks, and a scur of foam
White on brown, fringes the sun-bleached rock, in chains of cloud
As the sky moves over it ...
                     and I come to,
Walking back up the hill to get the minibus ...

As we drive to Langholm in its contracted grey
Through its empty main street
                     a green hill, rising beyond it,
Leans its summit to the right, and as the road climbs ...
The green, the green of it rising, going up into the blue
Up above a skirting band of pine trees at its base
Where a line like a path divides it;

All the shades of green: pine, leaf, fern and bracken
Interfused with grass, blending and distinct,
Blending, blurred out of the window ...
                     as we deepen among trees
– green of beech shot through with rosebay willowherb –

And we are on the borders of the Summerland
Where the dream of the ground is one with the sky
As the green is with the blue, where nothing divides it

A white Pan goat in the middle of a field
When I glance out, as startlingly white as a unicorn
With his twin horns, feeding, lowers his head,
The sky blue around him
                    the clouds puffed white-streaked and gentle
                    as gentle as living air, as gentle as breath

Now we closen ...

To where nothing in the green would suggest it
As we reach the turning ...
                        until we see the prayer flags
Lining the side among the trees, ruffling in the breeze.
Past the sign – KAGYU SAMYE-LING – we bump down the rutted
    track
Still wet after the rain, as the breath of them echoes,
Peace, stillness and purification like high altitude air;
Flat, on the level, we come round past cement mixers
And makeshift outbuildings to the front of the temple,
Over its sea of sand and sunlit gravel and mud –

And to think of it built by human hands dwarfs all perspective:
It stands like a crown, with its broad flight of steps
Leading up past the railings to two double red doors
Layered above the pillars with their insignia
Into a mosaic of red blue squares, oblongs, and gold
Above the windows with their mandalas to windows above,
And still more windows at the top above a disc like the sun
Supported by two llamas, their heads raised like lambs
To where the crown is a ship, an ark – come safely to land,
Suspended in mid-air, with its three tips like candles
Under the moving sea of the bright clouded sky

And the sun on the gold of it blazing like rain,
Golden rain from the source and the cause of all dreaming ...
We stand back amazed – it's outside all imagining –

52

And yet it's here, and our feet are on the ground.
We walk a little dazed towards the old Lodge
Past the peacocks feeding on scraps outside the kitchen door,
And inside, its worn interior like a fading drawing room,
At the front of the stairs we look for the reception
And you find the door into the office. We're told
There's still some lunch if we go through to the dining hall
And help ourselves (we can sort out rooms later –)
As I meet your calm receptionist eyes behind your typewriter
Shining and smiling with a light of their own
And I wonder at all they've suffered into light
So they can meet mine with nothing in between ...

And as we sit in the hall with its long wooden benches,
Carved back chairs, and huge thangka painting –
Woven in Wedgwood clouds translated into Paradise
In a lucid dream of serene eternal awakening ...
A woman with wild white grey hair marches in –
Wearing only a tattered blue dressing gown and slippers,
Hair loose, talking, talking out loud, talking to herself
As we shift and glance as if it's us (which it is,
Which is everyone listening, *I need to speak to you,*
I need you to hear me though there's nothing you can say)
And I notice some members moving calmly around her,
Too calmly, perhaps – as she rants out, banging –
As you explain, Yan, about compassion with your hands
And I wonder about her passionate rage ...

And when we walk outside, you arrive from Ardnamurchan:
'Hey Jenny!' 'Oh *there* you are' – late, but at last,
As if we'd just met in the middle of the Sahara
And you'd say the same, giving me the same embrace!
We decide to go down to the river to talk
Because we can't smoke here ... down among the trees
And its corridor of caravans ... to the boundary
Where the midges gather as we squat on our heels ...

And as the water moves with the swallows flitting over it,
And I watch them dip, curve, race, and glide
With the sound of the river in my ears, all I can think
(As you talk on) is *how many people are dying*,
So many people are dying, by the sound of the water,
So many are crossing the river now
                              beyond
Where a tributary comes to meet it, and the conifers mass,
Impenetrable to what is there in that bardo ...

I jot it briefly down, and the mist, the moment takes it;
We wander back to our rooms to rest before the lecture
And I dream of you, I dream and am empty ...

The sun gone over the garden, the coloured window frames
And the peacocks sunning themselves on the low roof
Turquoise and brown-grey ...
                              as we meet on the steps,
Go up to take our shoes off where the doors are open:
Inside, under the ornate lacquer roof with its skylights
And single chandelier, is the altar front
Massed and encrusted like a honeycomb, and in the centre
You, Lord Buddha, with your blue hair, eyes closed,
Cross-legged in a perfect body of awakening
That is golden, and yet human, and no golden calf.
What do the eyes say? Silence. Listen. And the hair?
You belong in a higher world. And the skin, the flesh?
I have overcome suffering. I am you as you really are.
And as the nuns move quietly with their cropped heads
And dark red habits, sitting and waiting
                              you come in, Ken,
In your brown velvet jacket, and without a word, without turning,
You prostrate yourself, holding your papers, on the ground.
I don't understand. Is it *thank you?* It is emptying self,
And you turn and sit facing us, ready to speak ...

54

The true world is made of cause and effect, you're saying;
It's not random or discontinuous as some would have it –
Although you don't judge … 'It makes no sense to them.'
Your voice quiet, clear, restrained, and observing
As you hazard how when religions are brought together
They're catalysed into examining their own beliefs
And it's not a challenge to anyone – it's the truth,
A truth that can be spoken the way you speak it,
Without any personal investment or trying to be right.

You branch into Hinayana and Mahayana schools,
Real things, ultimate and relative worlds
                                        but what I see
Is 'the mind knowing it's knowing', in the clear light
Where everything is mind and nothing is outside it
And inside it and beyond *is void*: this clarity
That is no difference between what I am and what I see:
And beyond our ideas of everything – *void*.
Cleansed of the reality it seems to have ('de-void'),
It's all here, all interwoven, all transient,
So stand in one another's empty shoes. We're one family
Naked with no clothing, and not a thought between us.
We are gold, as it all falls, and then there are no words
As you bow in your humanness, and you let it go.

You dedicate your work to the end of all suffering,
All sentient creatures, and 'all who are turned towards Reality'.
Lay down your cloak, leave as you entered –
Your ego a breath of silence on the wind
In the passing figure of your silence in the light
With your broad back bared like a heart.

And yet: *it's abstract*. When you ask me what I think
Something palls as I try to put my finger on it
As we stand on the mud-sand where you've gone
And I say I want a God that is rich and strange

Or I'd miss a God that is – since I believe Him –
Journeying through the alchemy of change
As deep as a sea in His Belly, as you knew him …

Where all this talk about cause and effect
Can sound like the nuts and bolts in a Mercedes;
And as it quickens as we speak I see it –
What I'm missing is the passion, is the *person*
(Take the passion away and the person evaporates)
As I think of You and how you stood
                    or as I see You
And feel You, as my heart beats … in mid-step

And while we sit eating and I watch
Two Tibetans in dialogue in front of the blue green thangka
 – one leaning back, the other pointing with his finger,
Gazing straight ahead of himself as he speaks –
Suddenly I'm in a tropical fish tank
Of colours and sounds, new colours and dreams
In the blue that transcends all my thinking, where *I don't know*
And a third stands with them (that's you, Julian)
And moves limping in a dark blue anorak like a shadow,
His angular head restless in silence …
Restless, questioning.

We decide to go out for an evening walk
Down the track to the gate and on to the lane,
John, Tom, Gilli, Michael, Jenny, and you, Gwyn.
As we walk, loosely as we are, in shifting combinations
We talk about dreaming, and you tell me your dream, Tom,
Of the Pope (no less) opening a door and inviting you in.
'What do you make of that?' *and it's your own authority*,
It's your change of life, you say, poised to resign,
And it's the dream welling up in you from underneath,
The dream that tells you as you dream your shadow
As I fall in step beside you, your face in profile,

Pilgrims on the road ... following the river below
That weaves and curves among overgrown banks.
We try to get down to it but the grass is too thick;
Hidden river, secret river of our lives ...
We surface and cross over the low pine-bark fencing
By a solitary green petrol station with its one pump
And bolted green shack behind it, like a hermit's hut.

And as we walk back you start talking about your father
You never knew, Jenny, since he left you as a child.
I see him in his youthful sepia portrait ...
And how suddenly you knew *he was in Middlesbrough*,
Suddenly you knew he was there when you asked
And the place name came ...
                                    and as we look up
The clouds are moving apart in front of us
And when I turn, for some reason, and glance behind
A jet trail is slitting its way across the sun,
Lit by the sun, its thread like whitening gold ...
You turn to me and smile, holding the silence

A lone blue tent down by the river,
Pitched apart, over the long rough grass field ...
And I think again of how it's all written on air,
The living air in front of our eyes, that is the poem
Unfolding step by step as we walk in it, and breathe it
Through the skein of our hearts as we see its blue canvas ...

We walk on a little way, leaving you by the gate,
And up a green grass mound like a little mountain
Surrounded by pine trees, where we find an altar,
A little stone altar seat, where we sit with the midges
And a cow in the field starts mooing loudly behind ...

We come back to make tea, and you tell me your story,
Marie-Hélène, as we stand by the kettle, waiting.

I notice *Days in the Sun* you're reading for your English.
You turn the cover up from your thumb –
And you talk in your slow clear enunciating voice.
You resist being called anything – 'I don't know' –
Even a mystic, when I ask you, that your hear as *mis-take*.
'Non, non pas de tout,' you laugh, and say 'I 'ope not'
And how you came here after collapsing with a migraine.
You woke up in Findhorn and thought *who are these people?*
Thinking you'd gone crazy, then were sent here to rest,
To a Christian monastery, you thought, but *what is this?*
'A Tibetan temple surrounded by green hills and sheep!'
I ask you if anything about it is déjà vu,
Trying to be simple, and you nod your understanding
But say, 'I don't know. It's like a dream – '
O brave new world ... that you could find yourself here
'For one month on my 'olidays', in perfect innocence ...

I go outside to breathe, wondering, and find her
Squatting by the work shed with its No Smoking sign,
Finishing one, naturally ... She glances up warily
Still in her gown, hair loose, her chin edges unshaven,
Red dye on her hands like blood, her fingernails caked,
And she asks me for a roll-up, and I do it silently,
Crouching on one foot, as the midges gather round us,
Striking the match, and cupping my hand
                                                        as she asks me,
'Have you been here long?' – sullen, irritated –
'I can remember when it was mud ... *mud*, all of it' –
As she drags on it, and I see the red in her eyes
And feel how she's been here from the beginning.
I suggest that Buddhism needs to return to the earth,
Expecting her to ignore the question, her face still down
For a moment, but then meeting my eyes she says,
'I used to think the earth was beautiful ...
Now I want to get off it' – and it stabs at me –

Off this whirling ball of mud, out of nonentity
And to hear her in the beauty she had, saying it ...

As she talks on fluently about 'matter-bound Gaia'
And Mother Nature that's no mother to her, but 'cruel'.
But what about the heart that transforms all of us
Linking us all and connecting us in our blood –
And Love? 'Well, it's hard to love people, isn't it ...'
'My partner drove me mad every morning with his habits,
So imagine trying to live in a community ...'
And I try to answer her, to reach her, but I can't
Because what she's saying is also the truth.

'And sometimes I hate, you know, I really *hate* –
It's awful, then it's over ...' She lifts her face
As I strike another match and rub at the midges
Biting for their lives, and we scratch our hair
And rub our palms as if massaging in oil ...

Only the story of you walking in the rain, Yan,
Suddenly with your shirt open, feeling it, speaks –
And she talks about the ego causing all suffering
And the suchness of rain, the wetness of rain,
As something gives
                                something begins to rain
Instead of all I'd want to give you.
I apologise and say, 'It's all so many words,'
And you say, 'Yes, so we can let them all go,'
Almost smiling across the torn wound of your mouth,
Or as near to as you can, as you stand –
And as I ask you your name, as you turn quickly to go

'Oh, that doesn't matter,' and the darkness takes you.

Day 7

Samye Ling

Muddled awakening ... in a shared room,
Cramped for space – for breath – for silence.
My companion lies flat out on his back, snoring
Breaking the grey light, and then the morning as he turns:
And where do you go in the night? Do you sleep? Do you walk?
I wish you peace in the caravan of your pain, Lady Ragnell,
Under the barbed wire stars like arc lights where there are none.

I head down to get tea, then get out.
Holding the steaming cup, I walk to the river
Where there's finally a moment of peace as I sit on my heels,
Finding my body beginning to sway, gently sway,
And then as it comes I'm singing two notes,
One high, one low – one for the light,
The other for the shadow ...
                                         as the swallows fly
Restless in their wings, never landing, they dip and glide
Like thoughts in and out across the screen of the mind

A mind that's never still
Till there is only the singer,
And I am only a witness to this moment, and You.

We gather back waiting for Yan, our shepherd
In his dark green anorak and soft pointed face
And his staff as palpable as air in his steps,
His deliberate Dutch voice, rounding his consonants,
As he gathers us up to lead us out to the lane and
Across into the field where the slow climb begins.

As we cross the grass, the herd, the entire herd

Of grey-black cattle and heifers in a line up ahead,
Begin to follow each other up the grassy tractor-track.
They turn and trumpet, opening their mouths wide,
Cows and calves and heifers, the whole family, like pilgrims,
Their booming roar ringing in its outbreath ...

As we follow them diagonally, climbing the grass
Towards the blue edge of air at its rim,
I glance down at wild flower after flower in close-up:
Yellow buttercups, white saxifrage and purple-mauve
Woven into the vivid green, while you walk up ahead,
Your body outlined in brightness like an aura
As you turn and look down, in your white-edged tracksuit,
Then climb higher and higher into the brightness till you become it,
Your name become translucent and silent ...

We reach the plateau, and I look down
Across the valley, the trees, and the temple roof glittering.
There's you, John, ascending slowly, bowed over your stick,
Your white head bare, on these last steps of your journey
And suddenly I see it's your whole life walking here,
Or any life, my life, as humbly as this
(Lest I forget –)

We stand on the plateau in the wind, the spring wind,
Spring wind of the earth with its flowers still blossoming,
The sun on our faces lit with the wind and grass
As we gather round – and you point out Ben Elkin
Over there on the skyline ... and the Ettrick Shepherd
Whom I see in your eyes as he walks alone
Up the length and breadth of the empty hillsides ...

When I mention saxifrage, you glance down in front of me
With your white head, unexpectedly –
Telling me it means *breaking the stone*

                                        as it breaks.

The shadow, all the heaviness, and my mind, breaks
As I stand with you and we examine the grass
Where a web beside the white flower is beaded in dew-silver.

We walk down towards the pilgrim river
In its aerial cleft, swirling between rocks among the trees –
Down from a rock pool you're saying you swim in,
In its green-tinged foam, where the salmon leap –
The salmon leap up
                                    their bellies glinting in the sun
As you jump in the startling laughing freshness of the water
In the naked joy of your imagining ...

We're walking now along Wild Water Byrne
 – called so because it plunges into the Esk –
As you explain with your hands gesturing your smile
(it plunges into the Esk, it makes love with the Esk
With the same wild light abandon ...)
We walk down an avenue of wild bright flowers
Planted by the fingers of the wind: purple colt's foot
And white meadowsweet in a litany of names in the grass.

And as we glance across the river to the other side
Three tiny Shetland ponies are gazing back.
The brown one comes forward while the black one stands
Licking the white one lying half out of sight behind the fence wire.

Such innocence you can barely imagine;
Such innocence you have to see with your naked eyes
In the joy of the day there is no other seeing in
Past the moment that is fading, and the memory stays
Half seen in the light as I look, and look again.

We come to the house with its delicate rusted gates
Open in the long grass among cowslips.
The larches stand in the glade, white flowers under them,

A carpet of white where the sunlight dapples
Shadowing white, gleaming on the flowers ...

And you catch your breath, feeling you've known the place,
And with such a strong feminine presence that is alive
The trees are like women, or witnesses to a woman,
Sophia of the larches, as I stand with her alone.

As we sit inside drinking tea and eating cake
In this old stripped-simple bare-boarded house
Unfurnished now except for the necessities ... looking out
Of the living room at the garden gone back to wilderness,
You talk more about Buddhism, seeing, clairvoyance
As I think of the Unknown Gospels in their desert jars
And you talk about the monk who after prayer and fasting
Saw a vision of the next Dalai Lama in the lake ...
In all that expanse of water, after all those hours,
I imagine him, dwarfed by the water, sitting, sitting,
Then, as the water opens up in a shimmering
Of the light on its wavelets, he sees – a face? A child?
Though how he sees, none of us here can explain
In the silence as you leave, and we leave it there
Like the light in the room as we stand to go.

As we walk back I keep seeing him sitting there
And remember waking one morning in Turkey
Far out in the Central Anatolian plain, in the savannah.
I see myself sitting by the edge of lake water there
In all that desert silence, under all its cobalt blue sky.
I can remember nothing, not even my own name ...

As we talk about the Rinpoche, and Krishnamurti,
Knowing and unknowing, and the truth as we live it,
I remember you, Jiddu, saying

'Truth is a pathless land ...'

Even though we know the way we're going back,
Even though we know the route, the whole map,
There are no straight lines, and then it runs out ...
(It expands, it enters another present dimension
Of grass and paths walked another way, as we walk now.)

We're back, and you're showing us round the workshops,
Past the Rinpoche, standing with his matching umbrella
Smiling in his robes, the *Compost Only!* sign beside him.
I look at our faces in the glass among the gilt eagles
In the full glare of the sun, white against the glare,
Transparent in our skins beside their beaked wings ...
And we go inside, to the main casting area.
A huge cracked Buddha-head stands on a table,
The bridge of his nose broken, like Ozymandias –
The fault line crossing under his inward closed eyes
Like an awakening, an eggshell swollen inside breaking:
'This is not my face. This is not my mind.'

As we sit back in the temple you talk about nothingness,
Trying to answer our questions with a patient ear:
Does transcendence deny the earthly? You suggest not.
You talk about his rising head and blue hair ...
We belong in another world, and yet we're here.
Strange paradox, which argument alone can't resolve –
Strange cross of ages there is no denying
And the shadow with its black occult underbelly
That led the left-hand way to the gas chambers ...

I walk down to the river for another break,
Meet you standing there, about to smoke too.
'I'm Colin' as you extend your hand, and I take it.
'You want one of these?' 'No thanks, mate, I'm fine.'
I ask what brought you here ... and you're saying,
'I knew I had to leave where I was. I didn't know where.
It was a bad scene; everything was going wrong ...

I even went to the airport, I was going to fly anywhere,
Then I thought of this place, looked it up on the map
And all I could see was the river, but I came!'
And then it happened, on the way
 – in case you thought you were in any doubt –
'Just as I was near the last train stop I was robbed ...
This guy said, "Give me all you've got!"' (inhaling sharply)
'I was so desperate to get out, I didn't care
 – it was like something in me snapped –
And I handed him my cigarette case and fifty quid
Which was all I had. "Have it!" I said.
That was the step, then I was out on the platform.'

So you let go of everything ... I'm shaking my head
Touched to the quick by your courage.
You'd even gifted your hi-fi to your brother before the trip.
'Everything. It was like *it had to be everything.*'
'So how do you feel here?' I'm asking. 'Safe – here I am.'
'This place is like a magnet, you know. It's strange' –
As I keep seeing you stepping out of that train ...
As we wander finally back up for supper.

I leave you in the library sharing your thoughts
On interfaith prejudice in the Church –
Before we gather in the temple, in a circle for ourselves
In the back room, again
                    in its deep clear evening calm
As you arrange the chairs round and we centre down:
Margot, John, Tom, Gwyn, Michael – all of us.
Glancing at your faces as you close your eyes
And, as I close mine, in the inner sky I find
In the sunset air spreading against the horizon
I'm seeing you all as birds
                         one by one, as swans
Silhouetted, black, lifting to fly –
                         one by one

Your wings freed into flight, following on,
Following each other in a long open line ...

And I would ask, would wish, nothing less for you, in love

And we wander on together, Gwyn, in the falling light
For the last of the day, down through the playground
Where the swings are empty, and we're slow to be children,
Slow to be free, large and clumsy as we are now ...
As we talk about the Wild One (Ragnell) and her suffering
That is the split between heaven and being here
And how we can't transcend without this, or we're in hell,
Lost in both worlds – as I see her.

We pass a field full of frolicsome cows.
'They must be Yan's,' you say as they closen
As if they've come to show us the answer
And one bounds over and sits, putting her ears back,
Looking at us as if to say, *'Don't you see it now?'*

We walk on, and talk about the birth pains
That we're all in, in this expanding.
I tell you about a woman I fell in love with
And it wasn't love but my initiation into it,
Hers too, like mine, into a *greater* loving ...
And though it hurt you, as it hurts me still,
I was learning there are things we can only understand
By being 'in love' that we can't grasp out of it
And how our freedom has to be to love, because it's *ours*,
Our love, ours – that we're all a part of
Even when it put me through the fire and burnt me,
Even though it was more like open heart surgery.
It was for all our hearts to be greater, the more
These arms were stretched, torn, between you

And, though it's easy to say, I hesitate
– God knows, it would be crazy not to –
I still half-hide my face, can't look you in the eye,
Knowing only 'you have further to go in love'
And that's maybe all we'll ever know – further, to the end
Beyond any rhyme or reason we can see
Because it is You, as it has to be

And your gift to me now is walking in wholeness
Being able to say these things, and freely.
'I'm walking in wholeness with you,' I'm saying
And no sooner have the words left my mouth, and we look up,
We're surrounded by the sweetness of curlews
Suddenly everywhere above our heads –
Filling the soft blue air, with so much space
They could fling themselves easily from hill to hill –
Sweet sweet sweet they call wheeling together,
Calling us to healing and this totality of trust.

We turn, and you talk about re-entering the dreamtime
As I recall you dying back into the mystery of being
As we pause by the pines, in their impenetrable shade,
And you tell me the moment you dreamt you were dying
Yet you were *waking up*, as you were ...
As I see you by those trees, as I will always see you,
Gazing among their brown fallen needles as you speak,
And your body on the ground is your body standing up
In the dream my eyes are seeing you in –
                                                this dream:

We return under the starlight, each star a Buddha
Somewhere in the after-echo of the temple gong
Shivering high in inviolate silver, raying out silver ...

And on the shadow of the ground as we pass
A single peacock picks among the bric-a-brac, in the mud.

Day 8

Lockerbie – Samye Ling – Milarepa

The sky like a great mottled cloud-filled pearl
As I stand, gazing up … beyond the river, above the trees,
The swallows, and the cloud of gathering midges;

Stretched like a sheet of crumpled drawn satin, so soft
It's the softest thing you can imagine –
You could almost wrap your eyes in it, and all your bare skin,
As you stretch to awaken under its spell of healing: *pearl*.

And I could not linger, there was only this moment of seeing it,
Seeing in silence, beyond words, seeing it whole
                                        and then, on –

The day gone so fast, already
We're driving you to Lockerbie, to the train
And pushing against time to make it –
Passing silently through this empty landscape
(Or as silently as we can bear not to speak),
This empty green landscape beyond the mere Christmas trees.
It dwarfs as it looms, swells, curves and rolls
As the road winds past slate-covered walls
As I turn the wheel
                    into the emptiness beyond –
The emptiness in the silence like a desert that is waiting;

Breaking, when we reach the outskirts of the town
And you glance at the invisible aeroplane crash-landing
Out there among the fields, larger than any of the houses,
Leaving the whole place cowed under its shadow: small and grey
And humbled with its funereal brick High Street we come into
Scanning for signs for the station –

And *why Lockerbie?* I keep thinking (as we all did)
And the sky has no answer,
Only the grey that is its pall-like colour

As we draw in to drop you, to park and walk in
Briefly to the ticket barrier while you wait at the kiosk,
And then it's like a dream ... the other kind of dream
When I blink and the room is empty, there's no one here,
Not even a scent or a presence in the air –
Only the door swinging shut. 'Bye, Gwyn,' you've gone –
Into my blood, into the brightness of my mind, into nothing

                                                    shunyata

Then we make the same journey back, racing to get lunch.

The guidance says 'be open to the pearl of the day'
When I sit at the table I've cleared to write
In the silent afternoon ... *be open to the pearl,*
That is being inside it as we are, under the sky –
And being open to the breath, to what wants to be
That is the Spirit in the breath of the day ...

And in what the Spirit wants to unveil, or make
In the silence between us where we give it space
Like a blank page that is listening, and waiting

As I glance outside at a member in an orange shirt
Who's delicately balanced as if on tiptoe, on a chair
That's on a twelve-foot-high trellis
                                        as if on air,
As if only the air is supporting him, and each precise
Movement he's making with the ends of his fingers
Working on telephone wire like staves above his head
While he balances to a hair's breadth

And a knock on the door echoes, and it's you, Jenny,
Bringing your poems, nervous before the reading
We're giving tonight in the back of the temple ...
You shuffle the pages on the edge of the bed.
We sit and look over them line by line
As I edit, sketching their shapes in the margins;
Line by line, as the sea breaks under those cliffs
Suspended as they poise without punctuation
And as they level the whole of Seaton Beach overnight
That you image as the leap of evolution ... ranged right
So the full force of the word hangs tidal, towering
In a void beyond water that is energy

                                        streaming ...

'Is/this my/world of stars?' you ask in the light of it
Bathing naked, as you stand clothed in the sun,
Clothed, unclothed, in *I*, before a face full of feeling
That is His, and your own: and then He is, you are, *there* –
There in the sunlight shafting through the window,
There beyond form and face, all Presence,
When our hearts open to receive You.

And say it as you feel it, as you first felt it;
Let the poem speak it as it speaks itself in you
I say to you (as I do to myself) so I can hear
The quickening of fire that is never sentimental,
Never merely poetic, or even 'poetry', but living speech
The way you'd say something for real you could never say
Or dare to, unless your life meant it –
And where there are only ears like that to hear you.

We wander down to the café and bookshop
And I find you there facing up to meet me: Milarepa
With your red mouth, earrings, and ruby saraband sash,
Your white transparent skin full of the snows of Lachi,
Sitting in a lotus spread above your demons

With its petals their colour, transmuted, become dakinis;
And the heaven of a pink sun behind you like a halo
As your fingers lean to rest against a blossom
And the mountains rise up like melting clouds into the sky:

But if you fear the round of birth and death
Abandon the Eight Worldly Reactions
Let us go to the snows of Lachi
Brother and sister, let us go to the snows of Lachi

Your face concentrates in repose,
And I wonder at the force of silence in you:
You lived what you were, you'd say, no more, no less,
By accepting all you'd been and all that came to meet you;
Those are your ornaments and that was your fuel –
Not something to be turned away from and denied.
You couldn't deny them, and they could disown you
In that cave of hell in Red Rock Jewel Valley
When they blazed like flames dancing around the walls,
Shouting *We are you! We are a part of you!*

And so you lived yourself inside out into your purity
 – with your pearl-white skin and discs for breasts –
That brought you beyond yourself, so you belong to all of us:
By living yourself, you transcended all self
And you sang the song of flame become serene white fire.

There is no reason to feel false shame
Therefore, Peta, do not create your own misery
Bring your mind back to its natural purity

It echoes in the air, in the living whispering air
As I come back via the office, where our eyes meet again
In a silent liquid flash of greeting and body.
I sit with the carpenter sawing away in the corridor

And my mind goes blank to its rasping,
Empty again.

And as I go to the river to meet you, Alan,
I see you as I saw you then –
Turning to meet me in silence with the water behind you,
Not speaking or saying anything,
But turning, in your anorak, the water twilight-silver,
Like a gesture within a gesture where the sound cuts out –

Or maybe it's as you pause, the way you talk to me now
In your quiet green detailed voice, as you show me
Your *Contract with Silence*, and I'm glancing over it
So as you pause and talk again about being here
I can see what you're saying: green stretches of fields
Where you're walking, nearby, past a century-old memory,
The scene of a local tragedy, imprinted on the air,
Engraved in your mind, and left to the wind
For you to witness as it is: life or death, as it is.

I think of how you honour silence
So as you speak, it speaks … like a vein or river,
A ghost-presence no louder than the rain
Or a leaf falling·suspended in mid-phrase.
'I'm pretty low-key,' you say, self-effacingly …

At the reading where we gather
And put the chairs out in a semi-circle, a half-moon crescent
With a thick white candle in the middle: it flows,
It flows like a river that is warmth, blood, and fire
As it rises, without straining, and quickens, catches,
Touching your face, and yours, and yours, in the light
That is our being human and sharing in this
Communion that is breath and bread for the taking.
'The poetry does not matter.' The poetry is a pretext
For what the air gives as we open to it: fire or grace,

Closening, healing, so we know who we are –
Who we really are, that we can speak of, utter
In your voice or mine, that is its sacred intent,
Its witness, vehicle and vessel: this body
Aligned in light as yours is, listening and feeling,
And the body we make together that is ours and nothing less.

I offer your applause up to the ceiling,
My hands open, holding nothing, none of it
But the heat I can feel in my palms
As we stand and sing: we sing for the earth,
We sing for the air, and we sing for ourselves in You:

Air I am
Fire I am
Water, earth
And Spirit I am

The whole art, giving it away ...

And the pearl? Came in an unknown hand
Out of the oyster of the evening air
Anonymously, on a tiny folded page
You handed to me smiling
As you shrugged, waved, and turned away ...
It says

> *the fire in your words*
> *makes my heart leap*
> *i recognise the light*
> *the eyes of hidden birds*
> *the sound of silent voices*
> *the voices that can speak*
> *the silence they will keep*

Day 9

Tibbie Shiel's – Glasgow

I come to the river, expecting the water,
To wake up, silently, and say goodbye to it –
And there's you, Silent One, standing with your back to me
Alone with your Walkman over your ears as you turn
Greeting me with your eyes half closed, your voice deadpan
In its monotone, your lips barely moving

And then, as if unsure what to say or do next
Other than smoke, as you turn back I ask you
To tell me your story, or what's left of it,
And as you talk of not knowing where to go next,
Whether to do the four-year retreat, or leave,
I see the truth you're saying and not saying,
That there's nowhere for you to go, no parents, no home,
So you're not cool, you're just lost, enormously lost,
Your eyes and your voice your only defence
While the hulk of your vulnerability opens and hangs
Like your bowed, bent back.

When you tell me you don't know who to trust
I see no one touches you – you're like a leper –
And I rest my hand tentatively on your shoulder.
It's almost too much; your voice starts to crack,
But you catch it back, clearing your throat ...
You need *her* to take you in her arms: and there's only this,
And the ache of knowing it could be too much anyway,
You'd only be abandoned again –
And all I can think of to say is
You need a home within a home, a *centre*
That's yours, and you nod ... and something of it stays

And as I step back, because I have to go,
You raise your hand in farewell, turning back to the water,
The river there's no crossing before it's time to Go Home.

I walk back up the path towards the farm
To find you, and meet you coming the other way
On your way into reception: and as we stand there
Suddenly without saying anything we embrace
And I'm holding you so closely worlds could pass between us,
The touch of you so unerringly completely familiar,
You don't need to speak either; *it's all been said*:
It's only when we break the silence and surface
I remember I barely know you and I hear my voice,
Then yours, making the distance we make

And it's like lost innocence, there's no going back,
It's too late, we've spoken of the fruit on the tree
We've eaten in the taste and shape of all we speak.
It stuns me – to see you on the Other Side
And to think of you, still standing alone
As your hand waves a trail like gossamer in the air
As you say goodbye at the end of the road ...

And as we gather to go, out of our rooms,
Standing around where we started,
You pass us like a gauntlet you're ignoring,
You pass by me without even seeing me –
Holding a teacup, in a dirty fawn skirt, walking quickly,
Shuffling in your slippers, your shoulders up, proud.
I watch your back until you vanish round the workshops

And the peacocks are down, picking at the bread ...

So much left unsaid, so much left unfinished,
Loose threads like strands of grey hair in a head
You have to dare to leave as they are

Because it isn't you who weaves them; we're woven in them,
In a timing and destiny beyond all we can see ...

It's your silence as it cuts and singes the air
That stays with me and becomes my own
Now we draw away down the muddy track,
Leaving the buildings silent and the prayer flags
Whispering on in the breeze ...

It becomes what's authentic, problematic, real
That cannot answer back in the face of suffering
With neat explanations or excuses —
That can only answer back with a compassion and a presence
That draws you in more deeply every time,
Until I see how it becomes the vow of vows
That grows in the silence, seeded in our hearts,
That takes a lifetime to take, that we are taking now.

As we drive along the road to Tibbie Shiel's
I glance sideways at your face, Yan, while you calmly explain
The error of planting Forestry Commission trees
In lines on the hillside ahead of us, so they bleed
The topsoil away, against the grain of the land —
And all for what? Quick profit. 'It's an outrage.'
'And are they aware of it?' 'Oh yes, perfectly well.'
For every thousand of them, there's one Ronnie Rose
(*Rose* — your accent inflects his R's
And his name warms and hangs in the air like hope)
With his wildlife restoration project, you explain,
Digging a pond especially for the deer and the birds.

We talk on about the meaning of psychology
And what it truly serves — and you ask me,
'What do you mean by the word spiritual?' I pause,
Taking your question in as the road goes past,
Blurs past, under the wheels, reaching ahead —

And I'm saying, 'I think it means *to go to the end.*'
You smile with your eyes as if to say, *'Not bad!'*
And then suddenly up ahead of us, as we slow,
Curled up in a ball halfway across the road
Is a hedgehog. You brake and step out and lift him up –
Run over, it must have only been minutes ago ...
And you bear him over to the side

And put him gently down in the grass ...
As you climb back in, there's blood on your fingernail,
Blood like rose, red as this moment's silence
And your hand carries it without wiping it off
As we round through Bowerhope up the side of

                                            St Mary's Loch

Spreading glass-grey under the green

          and the hazy white glare of the sky it reflects –

                 rippling in its wavelets

With *Summerhope* on the other side ...
The white of the inn closens, once a cottage,
Once her own home where the Shepherd met Sir Walter Scott
And exchanged tales round the fire, or so the tale has it,
You tell us when we arrive a thousand pages later.

And when we file into the main bar
There he is on the wall, etched in black and white
In his cape and sideburns, his hands folded,
His face trouble-free, free of himself
With what he knew out there when he walked ...
'Ye ken, he was an awfu' fine man,' she used to say

And here she is, years later, like a muse of stone
In her bonnet and shawl, her hands folded
Holding a book, mouth turned down and tight

At the love she'd had and never had, and survived,
Being mother instead, or sister, or maybe even lover
For one brief night in 1830 – who knows?
All you can see is the grief like a stone
Of a widow twice widowed, like a virgin to the end,
And *a queen*, they said, with Wullie behind her,
When all she had were her endless guests
And his statue with its 'clay-cauld likeness', for ever.

We get the drinks and sit, Ken
Talking about tradition and individual expression
In unbroken centuries of thangka painting
Where only the smallest details change
And the temple bell rings on into the snow,
Into the other side of silence and beyond
As the breath holds and the world stands still
Above the bright breaking ground of my faith
Where none of us know what to believe
But what we've felt and seen with our inner eyes
'And I don't know, sometimes, which I'd rather have.'

As the colours hang in the air, you tell me
About the aristo in the Botanical Gardens in Paris
You'd seen out walking, in his cloak and dressing gown,
In clothes he'd worn for weeks so 'he smelt like hay',
Feeding the pigeons, with the birds all over him,
Flapping on his shoulders and over his feet,
And smaller birds, jays, tits, all around him too.
'You couldn't see him for pigeons!' you say as we laugh …
You couldn't see Orpheus for the colours of the garden,
You couldn't see the song for the singer,
Or the dancer for the dance … and it breaks, and we
Know what we want: *epiphany – poetry – Revelation*.

We walk out towards the loch's edge
With ten minutes or so still before lunch …

Over the thin strip of land between the Loch of the Lowes,
Crossing a wooden bridge with no railings over a ditch
As I tell you about Parsifal: the two impossible bridges
He has to cross in faith before he finds the Grail,
Our feet slapping on the moving boards,
Which seem, for a moment, to sag at the centre.
Star Woman, where are you now?
With my heart burnt out like ash
What cloud have you gone behind like the moon?

What face is left inside the Rose
But my own heart now, and was it really you?

We stand quietly beside the vivid moving water
Eddying brown and silver
                          as my story falls away,
Then rippling – I point – and a fish breaks the surface,
Its belly bright silver, quicksilver
                               flopping over,
Leaving a wake of moving ripples that breathe
Into the stillness of our standing

And as I look out towards the other shore
Two white cars are moving apart, down the road,
As slowly as the moment holds

                to the slowness of the loch and the fell

                      etching us against the water

As a brown-winged, white-bellied dipper glides close,
Swaying up, down, and up with each beat of its wings
And I move my head to its rhythm
In a dance that is always dancing
From a stillness that is all-feeling.

Then we turn ...
And as you both walk on ahead,
Crossing the bridge with your hands clasped behind you
Poised in mid-step, where the centre dips,
I see you walking down centuries,
Attuned, step for step, in the brotherhood of your silence.

We sit for lunch where the old kitchen was
And you continue to tell me your story,
Turning, in your white shirt and bow tie,
As it comes to life, phase by phase in your eyes
And voice, softened by humour and shyness:

Dropping out of college, becoming a Chelsea beatnik,
And then travelling to Tibet in the late sixties
On the hippie trail that became something else.
'It was like going home, really. I couldn't explain
But everything else was an image that fell away ...'
And what did it? *This sense of having lived before*
That plunged you into the depth of experience
Behind all its façade — as it did for me —
'It was the only way I could make any sense of it.'

And since then? After meeting Katia ... clearance:
Seeing how all the past threads link to now,
A gathering of bright stained-glass shards
That bring us into the destiny of *this* life.
We agree ... then, when you tell me about her
And her long illness, you stun me to silence,
Half-empty plate and glass, everything forgotten,
Only her pale washed-out skin and bulging eyes
As I see the pain in your own:
'She asked to take all of it on —
All of her karma in one go ...' Almost unimaginable,
The courage and purity of that effacing everything
Until all I can see is a tallow-like glow

Like a chrysalis with its skin lit from within
(And will she make it?
                    Will she break free?)

We talk about karmic relationships, and the company
Of us dharma brothers and sisters, as it translates,
And how we outgrow each other to *it* – the We
That is being alone and together, that needs us
To be alone, be *I*, before we can be true to it.
I speak of your sword, Michael, cleaving the world
And the sword of truth we all carry, that is honesty
Plain and simple, unadorned … and miraculous
As the key to every shifting, living threshold
That only the truth can open, like doors in a dream;
Isn't that why real friends are so fearsome?
As every angel is terrible? That black voice at Duino
While I thought of you, Steiner, and what you died into
That was all of the struggle of your latter years,
Prophet of our time that we're living right now.

'Truly our friends are our most fearsome initiators'

And you nod vigorously, smiling …
We talk on about therapy and you tell me
About a woman who fell in love with her analyst
('He was also pretty much in love with her, too')
Who had the nerve to say, 'Look, why don't you calculate
How much all this is going to cost; then ask yourself
"Is it worth it?"' – and how that broke the spell,
Freeing her (and freeing him as well) –
And another woman he knew with a nightmarish room
She could never tidy up to meet the fire regulations,
So he said to her, 'Just make yourself a sign
Saying you're *about* to clear it up and sort it …'
And how that worked like a treat; she did it!
No more mess, and no more guilt and shame!

We laugh at his Zen arrow on target –
'And you know, he had a heart condition himself ...'

We look around, find everyone else quiet
– Tom folding his paper napkin, staring down –
In that pause before ending or grace, because it's time to go.
So we lay in our contributions, and stand ...

And, wandering out, there's you, Tibbie: one last time
In a framed plaque like embroidery on the wall
That tells us you were ninety-six and laid out in flowers.
'She was a good Christian' and maybe (who knows) a saint.

We stand around for a moment before boarding the bus.
I greet you with a final hug – 'We'll meet again' –
And leave you to walk away over the hills with Pomona
And you, Ken, to drive off in your metallic green Chevette,
A last wave of your hand – and you're gone,
Gone into the green of the Ettrick silence
Where the silence and the wind are as they always were,
Swallowing gently the revving fading of your gears ...

'Goodbye, Ken. And thanks, Mrs Shiel'

We drive on the other way, out to the mountain road
Winding round past Dam Top between two reservoirs
Flanking the sides like risen lakes.
The thin road narrows to a single-lane strip
                    of tarmac only six feet wide

And we are *on* the land, now
                    falling away either side

No longer surfaced above it ...
And we could be driving on the grass
Grass and stone is all you can see outside the windows

We could have left the road completely

A flock of sheep suddenly appear up ahead
Blocking our way, facing us like a protest
Of reincarnated Quakers! They stand their ground:
'It's our right of way,' as we laugh, and wait
Ground to a halt as they part round us like a sea,
Scattering behind us on the grass, complaining loudly,
And the shepherd looms up behind them, striding –

Then ahead, etched high on the sloping hill,
A rock crevice of pouring froth

                          spreading up like flame

White flame!
A flame in the rock, as if struck out of it –
Moses, John

               white flame of purity, ecstasy

And as we cross the brow where a stream gullies
Like the true path down, high above the loch ...
A shearing circle made of low stones between two walls
Reaching North and South as it speaks of the centre,
Its round shape anchoring the air

                     like a magnet

And our eyes as we gaze down:
'This is My Ground.'

Taking the steep road down, spluttering in second,
To where the grassy plain and the farm level out
By the loch ... and in all that expanse of water
Two old men with fishing rods, poised in an evergreen boat
Blending with the green, held in the breath of the stillness,
Rippling out to the farthest shore,
Waiting on the Lord

Waiting in the eye of Death and Life as you regard them.
'That's a nice way to spend an afternooon' (Linton)
Or hear your number called when your time is up
Or see them dissolving into the mist ...
Blink, and they're gone, the other side of blindness

As the land opens out like a book,
Like huge transparent pages of glass,
The height of the hills and the whole living air
You can read, sign by sign, if you will,
More lucidly than you can read these words:
Pilgrim reader, this is your lens ...

As we drive on to the flat where the tarmac is red,
Heart red, pink red, on the road to Biggar

                    where the plain of the Lowlands opens out

And the wheels thump down and echo,
And we're on the road now, the road of our choosing.

I drive in silence (Tom navigating)
Taking the last three days in –
Fixing these last images in memory,
Seeing them again until they become feeling
Reanimated inside my inner sky
Even after pages of intervening grey
Sleep, oblivion, forgetting ...

Grey, as we head to Glasgow, driving fast to make the time,
The land blurring past towards the city's outskirts,
Eaten up, mile after mile, by buildings,
Roads, streets, traffic, and lamp posts
– the sounds and smells all changing –
And it's like the edges of Carlisle, only worse

The shock of these drab council houses and tower blocks
After the wind and the green heights; staining the eye.
'No one should have to live like that – '
And you say, 'They're all falling down anyway ...'
No, gives us houses made of wood, from real trees;
Give us the right to build, the right to breathe.
Babylon a rat-trap starved of bread and water
Designed by architects with their heads in clouds of lead,
Saturnine slaves, devouring their inmates ...
Fed by bitumen and tar

We leave the M8, following the signs to Cowcaddens,
Weaving through the rush-hour streets to Woodlands
As you pore over the map like a worm-cast
And the lights and horns pour round us in a dream
As we sit in the buzz and glow of it. *'What's happening?'*
'What's happening tonight?' 'Is anything happening?'
'Rosemary and Alasdair are giving us a meal,' you say
And we catch the sign to Hillhead and settle back
To the last of the plush red Victorian streets
Where the buildings tower, near the university,
Before we reach the International Flat.

Street parking – *stretch, uh!* – rescue baggage,
Climb unlit stairs with old girder rails.
Welcome at the door, and pour hazily in
Like beings from another planet, these pilgrims ...

Sitting in the lounge, I note the gist of this
While you bring in plates and light the branched candelabra
You've found, Margot, with its seven thin holders
That bring back the synagogue as you place it dead centre.
Voices – feelings – stories and impressions,
A conversation I'm too tired to remember,
Then slowly the room empties, armchair by chair,
Slowly the room becomes my own

As I'm left alone in this chair I'm sitting in,
Everyone scattered over the city to our different nests,
Only the minibus keys to remind me.

It's a two-day city retreat, and I need it
And I need the touch of your hands in the twilight
In the street light filtering through the curtains
With the oil of geranium under your fingers,
Your close-pressed soft massaging fingers
Breathing over me and vanishing as I sleep beyond desire.

Day 10

Glasgow

W aking ... dream phrases ... whole sentences, or lines
That vanish, that break into silence once spoken –
'Feelings without words', or feelings beyond them
In the traces they leave as they disappear ...
The almost-ache of feeling for something beyond reach
You gave and then you took away,
And is this how You want me to feel?
And was it you, even before you came?

'Without fire, you can only speak so long,'
And then water: so the dream voice tells me to feel,
And then air: to think with, into clear space,
'And without earth you cannot feel at all.'

Fire, earth, air, water:
And then behind my eyes, and between them
 – as clearly as if it was in front of them –
A shallow crystal wine glass

                              empty, so as to receive

Its tall thin stem
In the glowing silver light

The finest of impressions

                         shining down like moonlight

Like woven strands of white hair
Falling down around it
Framing a woman's face

                         come out of crystal

A beautiful nameless face beyond words.
(And was it you, was it you, Kilmeny?)
And the glass? Was to catch her tears
As the most precious distillation ...
Now I lift the glass within and drink them

And they find their way down in me, they loosen me,
They move into my jaw and in my heart
As the bulb of my lower body stir and swells
And I cover it over in plastic glass briefs

in *Glass Gow*

City of Glass,
And I come to what the inner man requires.

You come by for lunch as I surface, with Michael,
Your glad-awake voices three times louder and faster.
'There's a café down the road. It's a short walk from here.'
We emerge into the sun-struck street, past Sardinia Lane,
The name painted white on the brick like graffiti –
Its cobblestones leading into a tunnel of trees, invitingly,
Where we come to *The Underground* (the other kind, supposedly),
Down its short flight of steps, below street level,
And in through the swing doors littered with posters
To the cool spotlit semi-wholefood interior.

We queue and sit

And I glance at James Hogg
– a far cry from these arty Cement Garden walls –
As you talk about Steiner and the Paradise of poetry,
Which means hard work as Cecil Collins stressed.
It's so much easier to think in grey, and dream in it,
Confusing your dreams or your realism with reality,
And yet, I'm saying, as I recall rewriting 'The Rock'
– weighing down this rucksack beside me –
Draft after draft because it wouldn't come free,

I found a secret locked in its impenetrable air,
Which is that when a poem is difficult
That's where I need to learn to break its flow
To let the Spirit in beyond my will and control;

So grey is for graft, mystery of the number 8,
And what flows in us underground in the basement.
And as I glance over your shoulder at the wall I see him

Postmodern Man, asleep in a bath, like Chatterton
Naked, with his grey mask in his hand dangling
Where his arm leans out over the side ...
And the paint on his arm is peeling, strangely cleansed,
Lulled in the steaming grey-white water ...

As a woman leaves, tossing her long blond hair,
Reflected for a moment in the glass of the door,
Her willowy body in step with her stride

        as he sleeps

And when we come back to the flat, and you leave, I find her
Rising in my mind, in the silence

For Kilmeny had been she ken'd not where;
And Kilmeny had seen what she could not declare;
Kilmeny had been where the cock never crew,
When the rain never fell, and the wind never blew,
But it seemed as the harp of the sky had rung,
And the airs of heaven played around her tongue,
When she spake of the lovely forms she had seen,
And a land where sin had never been —
A land of love and a land of light,
Withouten sun, or moon, or night;
Where the river swa'd a living stream,
And the light a pure and cloudless beam;

The land of vision it would seem,
A still, and everlasting dream.

She blazes in the colour of the air
As softly as a whisper, as if she was sunlight
Slanting through the window lighting up the dust
Behind me, as if she was here.

She fills the room, and my heart, as if she was here.
She is here.

She is here, brightening and fading ...
It was you, reaching me before time ...
And I reach the piano and play for you

                                        in your long after-echo

Feeling for the notes as they come,
Following the music my fingers already seem to know,
Reaching for you in the high notes, that are yours,
As the scale rises and draws the depth up to them –
Following you through the realms of Light,
Seeing with the lion what you have seen,
That there is a Kingdom and it is here,
There is a place where the light never goes down.
It sparkles in the leaves; it glimmers in the shadows,
In every living breathing thing, where we will find you;

Kilmeny, Muse-Mother, Feminine
Anima beyond the grave,
And the mystery of you is this: *you are in me*;
You are the woman my heart yearns to meet.
'It just has.'
                        And you are the yearning, the loving
That opens my heart to The Pure:

'I am in every woman's soul.'

And when I turn on the piano stool I am alone.

Sleep.

I lie back now, eyes closed.
You work on my feet with your practised fingers,
A musician plucking a silent cello –
And I feel who you are in what your deft touch knows
Unlocked from your mocking, self-mocking shyness
That shadows your face as you press and probe
Among the nails and thorns of bones there ... Michael

Thanking you as you leave me with the curtains drawn,
And I hear it, drifting into my mind –
'You are the glass'
– even as the kids play outside
Over on the swings,
Their bright voices shouting *woh, woh, woh,*
It doesn't break:

*'The vessel is filled
and the Drink creates ...'*

As you drift back, Gitta Mallasz, talking with angels in the night.

We work now by more than daylight;
The candle you've lit on the low table flickers.
It's like working in glass, into the fine sense of your tuning,
Notating it line by line into its shape on the page ...
Blown from within, as its bulb expands
Around the breath of your lips as they move
And 'It's so fragile,' you say,
Taking each pause and stress behind the words
to their Source

Where the lines of a hollow cross
Meet at their centre:

You see the spire from your Devon window the sun pours through,
And you were the vessel the words came into
As the sun shatters the silence around it,
Shatters it in silence to the cry of the desert man,
Ablaze with light as the spire holds,
Your words hover, and blaze, and hold –
And John of the Desert is here in your eyes

Purity of being, purity of desire,
And it's *you* I want to feel, it's your fire
That tells me who I am and where I'm from
Down a tunnel of centuries, tempered, from John to John
Mysteriously transmuting, *Beloved and Baptist as one*,
And you tell me, 'You don't see yourself with all you give.
You don't see the light radiating out ...
All you do is drive yourself into the ground.'
I shy from its implication, and inflation

But all I can say is there is a feeling of him
Beside me, *as an other one and an inner one*
Walking cleanly through the middle of my 'home',
My 'work', all the self-definitions of my ego,
And he isn't interested in any of that
As I become him; none of these things matters,
All that matters is *him*, as I walk towards him

And yet you say, as I walk I *am* him,
I walk towards You, yet You say I am You

                                        and then?

I become an 'I' that is no longer self-conscious,
I become I AM, as you do — we do
As it hovers in the flame and its glow on your face

I forget myself, and I speak in Your Name.

Day 11

Glasgow

*Y*ou said, 'Remember your dream' ... and it was him
Focused in the centre of the picture: the pilgrim –
We were coming together on the rim of the landscape,
On the edge of a hill *where the glass gave way to the land*,
Transparency to earth, to dreaming earth ...
On this Sabbath morning in Glasgow, meaning

'dear green place'.

Then you call in, Harriet, after you rang
From two miles away across the city –
And it's great to see you. We remember singing
All together and the harmonies filled the air above our throats
And open arms as we sang on and on ...
But I see a shadow cross your face. I ask how you've been.
You pause and look down, your face changing
And all the song seems to dissolve in pain
Now you tell me about Ian: you visibly age ...

His absent father, introversion, and then violence
After coming back from Canada to find the same agony:
Throwing a bench in the kitchen clean through the window.
You watched the glass shatter, helplessly scared –
The wounding of your family tree, and your journey
To return to where you left him and reclaim yourself ...
As you send an art therapist in through the back door
Near where the window smashed you wonder what it will take
Before they realise 'it's the symptom, not the cure'.

And to see what we're breaking down for,
To touch bedrock, the rock there's no evading,
For all of us now, returning to spirit,

To return where there's nothing left but it,
Because there's nothing left, so we can see it —
And it has the space to enter us, becoming us ...
I share my memories of Oxford, and how
I was broken down to utterance, to words that were real,
As I returned from silence to language, back to a voice
Meaning who I am; and so these words have meaning, too.

As your suffering hangs like smoke in the air
Where the sunlight was, past your going
I pray for you with all the fire I know:
May all her shattered rage heal
And her heart become immortal fire,
Become that fire rising in her son
And the void of the blank page yield you colour
Even in your first unknowing marks ...

May all violence become its antithesis, Creation.
Creative rebellion, we need you!
And smack in the face of the Father, so He can heal you!
Tell Him what you fucking well think!
Or the sky and the trees will no longer exist.
Creation. We need Creation, as we need You.
Give us the voice to say it —

And when you drop by on your way back to Ardnamurchan
We eat together and I share the heat with you,
Then wave you away, laden on the stairs:

'See you on the island there!'

And just as you've gone and the sound of your engine's fading
A fire engine comes racing up the narrow wet street,
Blue light flashing, and a car alarm bleeping.
It hoves into view, raw pillar-box red —
Racing to the blaze, speeding through the wound,

And the air breaks with the sunlight gone ...

                              into soft rain

Soft Sabbath rain, and the sound of tyres hissing,
As the day comes back to itself.

I think of you, across the air
Miles away on your crowded Stroud green hill
Where the valleys swim beneath you out of your unicorn gate,
And I tell you

I don't know what's in me
It has no name
But I'm going to the place
To the rock where I will stand and wait

And as I think of you, dear one, clearing the attic,
Ferrying car load after load to the dump,
All I can say is all I ever could and shall,
Learning to live to the ends of my fingers,
Descending into my innermost being:

And the knowing is Love
And that we are the source
Let nothing come between us
And its clear bright water ...

You have all I have, on my way to the Man.

And Fire becomes Love in the rain, the soft rain.

It's time to walk

                  – skirting the edge of the pavement,
Past the railings ... and the lines of parked cars,
The air grey and quiet, no one else around

As I reach the end of the street and cross the road
Where a white-stained domed building stands shut.

I don't know where I'm going; I veer right
And find the park, with its long-drive—gate entrance
As if to a non-existent country mansion ...
Where the paths are still wet black tarmac, like the road
Reaching over a stucco bridge that crosses the Clyde.
I hear the homing call of a woodpigeon,
Secret to itself in an invisible tree,
Wrapped in a cloak of rain it is as soft as.

I pass the statue of Carlyle, and the soldier
On its rough plinth of unworked rock – *prizione*
Where what comes from the rock is not eternal
But mortal flesh and faceless, inflated stone –
Set in the shadow where they strangely leave nothing
But dumb silence as I cross the bridge and turn
Back to where they're human-sized on the other side
And a black spire rises above the trees, and them,
Hollow above its arches in the air,
Vertical to its three points like a triangle,
Soot black under the grey-white sky.

I turn to the path, and a man up ahead
Is feeding the ducks with one foot on the railings.
He breaks the bread, and they gather around him
In silent communion as the food leaves his hands.
He doesn't even turn as I pass him, intent,
Him in his silence, me in mine,
And there's nothing to say but what he's doing ...

Just beyond him, a gang of woodpigeons
Cluster on the overhang of a bare-branched willow
They blend with in sadness past their song
Where the branches of a sapling open out,

And I glimpse the detritus clogging the river ...
Cross on to another bridge, and lean over:

Gazing down the stream curving towards a brick arch,
And own into the water at an upended tree
Returned from the concrete world, useless, finished –
A bright orange bollard, snagged, facing down,
A rusting square like a lobster cage, half submerged,
Driftwood and hardboard torn and sodden
Drifting down the green river, from the green dying sea;
And in all the tangle of nettles and brambles
On the bank, a single giant hogweed,
Its centre surrounded by eight white blossoms,
Its green centre, the rose of the green:

Glasgow, look to thy 'precious green'
In this year of your celebration –
Your river is choked with offal like a lie
As you advertise your glory on the buildings above ...

And as I walk back the way I've come
Past the blackened Regency facades and littered streets,
As the light begins to fade into a deeper rain-grey
Of grief or lament – I find a brick wall
Where the writing is criss-crossed in white
Following the ruled lines the bricks have made
And I slow my eyes letter by letter to decipher it:

ITS TOO BIG TO STOP
IT'S A WAY OF LIFE
DON'T LET THE BASTURDS
WEAR YOU DOWN

Its angry shout of despair spraycanned in the silence,
Its truth burns like glue in my mind,
And my heart says there has to be another way

Over the dreaming tower blocks in the ghostly grey ...
There has to be another way, and we must find it.

As I climb back up the stairs I meet you, Grace,
With your smiling African face, fine high cheekbones,
Emerging from your room where you've been working
(Toiling away to finish your thesis ...)
While we stand in the kitchen, you tell me;
We laugh beyond all its abstractions when you say,
'Life begins where an economics thesis ends, hey!'
And in your mind's eye all you can see is a plane
As you spread your arms – 'Freedom!'
Silver-winged, bearing you back home ...

And when you all arrive back in, each bell ring
Filling the room where you stand where the space was,
My retreat ends – and we make a circle
Of chairs and light the Jerusalem candle,
Leaving one empty for you, Val,
Like an invisible guest, and we sit in silence
Wondering where you are and I half-hear your voice,
Lost pilgrim, struggling for connections in the night ...

We decide to leave you a note and go on
With the directions we're following, down to Jo's Garage,
The only restaurant nearby open on a Sunday.

We follow the street down in a loose file ...
It opens at the edge of the traffic and the lights,
Like the belly of a city, submerged in itself ...

We sit at two tables pulled together
In the garish pizzeria bar-room light.
I'm sitting with you, Josephine, sipping cheap red wine.
With the din of our talk around us
I have to strain to catch what you say, or I'll lose it,

Leaning close, half-closing my eyes, listening
To your still small voice at the centre of the storm
Telling me about your previous journeys like lives.

You tell me about a man who visited Assisi
And met a guide in the church door in a cassock,
'A saintly man,' he said, who showed him all round.
Then later – when he met the sacristan –
He asked him, 'Who was that?' and saw him dumbfounded.
He said, 'I'm sorry, but there's no such person here,'
And you smile and say, 'I think it was St Francis,'
As I draw breath in the brown of your eyes ...
Who dies, when the word of God is here?

You tell me how you came to England in '73
And how your husband died, leaving you
To raise your three daughters on your own.
I ask you what they're called, and you name them,
In Hindi, as you did – 'for the Glory of God',
'For Faith', was it? – and the last, 'for Compassion'.
Definitely, compassion ... as they open like flowers
And I think of all the hardship you've had
To still call them by those names, under a blank racist sky,
And your voice opens my heart to who I am inside it.

Then you tell me your credo: 'God is within you.'
'We don't believe in sin ... that's separation.'
And I see us again *'Trailing clouds of glory*
From God who is our home', and home is *here* –
Here in my heart, you say, as you gesture it.
'God is in your heart, and in your breathing,
No further out than the furthest star ...'
He is here, He is heart, He is Almighty Heart.
As your eyes shine you add, 'He is bliss ...
The whole point is to shed the layers and reveal Him,'
And I see the nakedness you mean –

I feel it between us as my heart becomes my skin.

Then you enquire courteously, 'What is your own idea?'
And only the truth will do; 'I don't know.'
'I know the Son,' I'm saying, 'but not the Father.'
'But the Son will lead you to the Father?'
As I stare down into the grain of the wood ...
'Yes, I can feel He is in me too.'
'Yes,' you say, 'it's your Self you're going to meet,'
Giving me this gift, and its mystery
When you add, 'Every person's path is unique,'
Every step, uncharted and unrepeatable,
And I think of all the steps we've been.

Surfacing, I come to your eyes, Tom.
You talk about the need of definition for dialogue
Where interfaith is: 'Or it's just so amorphous'
– world-weary with your knowing – 'though at the same time
It's a personal intuitive thing, not intellectual.'
Thank God, and it's not your job, but your journey –
And John chimes in with his Quaker Universalism,
Wanting the *Gita* along with the Bible on the table.
Tom says, 'But then it's not Quakerism anymore,'
And we smile up the nose of their rising disagreement ...

You weigh in with your definition of 'atheist'
Then 'agnostic' (meaning positively uncertain),
Ask me what I think, and I say, 'Mystic.'
'Ah yes,' you say as we gaze like wondering fish.

You tell us, Tom, your story of the Jesuit
Who went to study Buddhism, had to lay aside
All he'd learnt, and taught in the seminary for years.
After they told him, 'You're too deeply Christian;
You'll never understand Buddhism,' his faith began to wane.
He went back and back again till none of it was left,

And then *'out of the ashes of my faith, Christ rose'*.
He came back –

I know how you know it before you even say it,
As something gathers and reddens in the air
Like your face, Tom, when you say you saw Him –
Your heart opening, your eyes shining
As you say, 'So I knew beyond all doubt ...'
And you look down for as long as the silence hangs,
A shy lover who's blown his cover

Naked and then unafraid ...
And I see it's there, *there* we are pilgrims
Beyond all definition, where we walk through all of them
And all our differences, until we become ourselves,
To the only place we can go, where we meet
As red, unafraid, and as unashamed as you;
That's the place.

I turn to you, Christine, with your silver-white hair,
Eyes shining like your name: Christ in you.
You tell me about the rebirth of your local church
In Selly Oak, as your own – in your own body –
And it's the church we make between us
As we understand each other in more than words,
Or age, or dialect, as we overlap ...
And overlight each other as we see

And as we walk up the length of this silent dark street.

Day 12

Glasgow – Murdock Country Park
– Campsie Fells – Dunblane

A wedge of light …
                        waking me,
        Crossing the room through the nylon-veiled curtain,
        Slanting over my thighs, and drawing me
To kneel gazing out through the low sunlit window
Where it gleams on the stone of the building opposite
Beyond a screen of hanging branches dappling it with shadow –
Rising to the cobalt blue of the sky the windows' glass goes to …

And I go downstairs to the breakfast room,
Sit at a single table, poised as if to write,
And the light
                        brightens behind me … as if through crystal
Through the white of the lace curtains and among us as we eat,
Touching our faces, the cereal packets, and the plates
Silently while we bathe in it, hushed as if suspended …
The light
                is stronger than the radio and the high-speed doom
Of the 9 a.m. news with its dead flashes of speech –

And when a woman's voice sings
                        without my even hearing the words
The rhythm of the song becomes fire
                        tingling down my spine, like fingers …

The light
                warming over us, like a wave,
And on to the blank double page of this large black notebook,
Etched through the lace
                        criss-crossing over its lines

In a filigree of moving illuminated shadow ...

And Kilmeny is in the light, and is the light
   The light of a thousand pure-bodied women
      Streaming in veils and nakedness
And it is the same light
                              that shines through your smiling eyes
Before a word was written

And now you stand outside the front door
With its green-framed sign IONA GUEST above you,
Flanked by two hanging baskets; in your tiny blue tracksuit
With your hands crossed and your mouth horizontal,
The luggage at your feet half up to your waist.
The song begins
                  somewhere above my head:

'California dreaming ...

Drifting out of an upstairs window behind you,
The volume turned up. I lift my eyes to the roof line
And the sun bounces off a high window
                              under the free transparent sky

on such a dreamy d-a-y ...'

My legs and feet begin to move,
Itching to move, to breathe it in,
To dance three steps on the spot, to sway to it,
To raise my hands and arms if I could –
And my eyes flood with light and blueness
                              at the joy of it

As you smile and say, 'I think it's done ...'

We walk on down the street, I carry the luggage
Round the corner, as it plays out and fades,
And we come to where we're gathering, outside the flat.
You're there to see us off with your priest's car, Andrew,
And as I lean in to say hello to your wife,
The seat tilted back beside her, from out of the shadow
Appears the full face of a Child of Light.
'This is Matthew,' she's saying, *and he knows me.*
He doesn't even need to say hello as he gazes
Steadily without moving, as his eyes hold mine,
Their brown depth knows as they shine and we smile,

And when I stand back *it's the same love*, again.

Linton is fussing over the map,
Certain he knows the best route, determined to navigate
Wedged in the front seat. Tom pulls a face,
Not trusting his sense of direction, and it's farce
Except that it *proves* we are all children ...
And who cares anyway if we get lost? 'Come on, John,'
It's a beautiful blue day and the hills are waiting
As we pull out, his finger poised on the page ...

Smyly is talking about children in Africa
As we weave north, leaving the city behind
Drawn out into the blueness as if by the sky.

And as I gaze up
                two jet trails intersect
In a floating flat cross in the expanse of air –
Inked white on blue, shredding, like roads of cloud

            after the motorway has gone.

And close to the ground –

a lithe horse, its brown coat shining,
Its head bowed over beside its forelegs, standing by a gate:

The cusp of the land

        rising again …

As we round the edge of a field of sheep,
Suddenly on the right – in the middle of nowhere –
A woman in a pink jumpsuit, hair in a white headband,
Is standing with her hands behind her back, gazing forwards.
I blink and look again, disbelieving
As if I was dreaming and she was not really there

Like a being from the future,
A civilised, healing future
Where everything is possible against the screen of this air,
Whose blueness brightens

          as the road winds on

Until we come to the sign for Murdock Country Park
And we drive in past the cafeteria complex, to wait.

Summerland light, and the past is a shell
Where the wet path leads among dank trees
And out into the sun drying the heavy ground,
Where a brown heifer grazes under the shade of an oak;
And the facade of the building with its battlements
Above vacant window spaces overgrown with weeds,
Nettles, brambles, and tufts of high grass
Cordoned off with wire … and if the lords were here
They are long gone into this rotting leaf mould
And evaporating air: this place is for crows, and rain,
Glooming, lowering grey sky, intrigue and murder:
Under the blue air it simply looks absurd.
'What are we doing here?'
'I don't really know. It was John's idea.'

We walk on, in among more trees,
With mosquitoes and stubbornly sodden paths,
Out to where a Norman tower rises
Blind, with its eye slits closed, behind a gate
We clamber vaguely over, looking for information;
The book has closed, and the past leads nowhere
But back in a looped circle the way we came.

How long will it be before we see this past is over?
In a light that casts no shadow against the blue,
That a woman weaves in and out of like air?
There are no ghosts here, no glass, and no memories
But what is living in the light, and is alive.
The judgement is life, or the lack of it — the life
That is the Spirit assuming visible substance,
Source of all colour, all grass, and all eyes …

We drive towards where the day goes

                                    rising

With the curve and grain of the land

    (north towards Strathblane now …)

  in its sunlit greenness stretching   under the sky

In eternal summer light behind my eyes

Where the years are one — and there is no time,
Only the whisper and the breath
Of the light blazing down,
Where we remember what it is — and we remember
That this is where we live,
Where we are closest to where we came from,
Seeing this is all we'll come to

                and what we'll become

– like coloured figures hand to hand across a landscape –
Or like flares of curving light

that are part of the light

And the ground, and the air, and everything that surrounds them.

I think of you, Bill, and I think of you, Frances ...

And on Campsie Fells there is no death
As we wind up via Haughhead –
And park in an open lay-by while we stop for lunch.
We wander over to eat our sandwiches by its edge,
Sitting and looking out towards the valley cleft
Descending and rising on the other side
– descending and rising as part of one rising –
Where the green of the trees blends with the grass.

And just as we're about to leave,
As you stand with the blue of the minibus behind you,
Its side door open ... you tell me, Christine,
With the sun in your eyes and your face in the light
About your friend Ellen and how she died;
How a door of light opened for you, as it did for me ...
And the light seems to brighten behind you, and in you
There is no death, do you know it now?
As I gaze beyond you at the ridge of the fell,
The spring wood rising, the light at all your edges,
And above you, above us – look,
A single blazing white soft cirrus cloud
With its combed woven streaks, in a space between the others,
As white as your hair, and your liquid blue eyes
Bringing tears like light to my own
As we meet in silence, silence that is light.
I thank you, then, 'Thank you for reminding me.'

We drive over and down

        off the route, near Fintry

The flock gathered in the heat round the roots of a tree,
Lying down, panting ...

And into Carron Valley with its planted pine expanse.
We draw off the road near the reservoir ...
Where the track leads into vivid inner evergreen.
In we walk, up its bleached sandy length,
And I walk with you, Christine, wanting to be silent:

This is the Summerland; we have walked through the door.
Oh be silent, I want to say. Don't talk, just be here,
Or if you have to, at least talk quietly ...
See the cones high on the trees like candles
Catkin-yellow where the sun gleams on them against the blue;
Decorated, dressed, burning in soft silence
As we pass them, following the path to the end,
Walking slowly, wondering at the light with each breath
That so gladdens your eyes in their seeing
Where air and green and pine scent are one being
Saying *sense* and *celebrate us* as only quietness can ...

We follow on, left, where the path peters out,
And left again through the long wet low bright grass
Between the trees we have almost to wade through ...
Follow, though you don't know where it will lead you.
You are safe in the Summerland, safe beyond your knowing.
Come in among the trees down an old logging track
Where the ferns and brackens are as thick as pillows
In the emerald light, cool as if to lie on.
Lie down, and the forest will give you healing.
Lie down and shed your clothes to its blessing,
To its living sleep where all your dreams will return.

And how do we get back? We turn,
Lost for a lingering moment: 'Is the path left or right?'
I say *left* because I want it to be again
And it turns out *right* is the safe way home
 – the easy way, as we breathe, back on time –

Back early, and the breath of it hangs unfinished
While I stand by the reservoir become a lake of blue ...

And as we drive on

                        you point out the Trossachs on the skyline, Tom,

Over a vista of fields and light green, becoming trees
Where the earth is dreaming ... as they rise

                                            in soft purple slate

Slate mauve, with the clouds above them

                                    – like a screen of pearl

Hung with the blue and the white of them interfused ...

And you say to me, whispering inside
At the fine edge of inaudible thought,
'Walk in your own purity
Don't try to take everyone with you
You are all where you are meant to be'

 – the hay being harvested either side of the road –
While you women bow asleep in front, your heads moving
As we closen to Dunblane
                        the clouds gathering

High and rain-edged across the sun

– O light don't fade –

And we approach on the last of the motorway
And into the late afternoon quiescence of the town,
Heading up the main street towards the Cathedral Square
As if spiralling round increasingly to silence,
Invisibly as we climb, to where it looms huge,
Dwarfing the roofs below up the length of its windows
To its stunted spire like a knife-sharpened pencil.
We come into the shadow of its walls like a brown cowl,
Cloistered, ghosting the air, like its bell ...
(with St Blane and Bishop Clement buried in the ether ...)

And as we disembark by Scottish Churches House,
Its block of cottages flanking the altar end,
The bell chimes in the sun, counting six to its echo,
Fading up into the mountain and the gold light above it.

At the supper tables the sunlight holds
Like the silence as it streams into the room
And we talk about our names, because you said,
'You will come to Christ through your Christ names.'
Echoing in my mind ...
And in each of our names: a space for the light
In the silence after we speak them ...
You smile, Christine, meeting my eyes as you say,
'People always used to call me Chris before I realised.'
Some of you looking down, some of you wondering
As I wonder: do we *want* to be our names?
Do we want to be our secret selves? Do you?

And you walk in out of the light
 – you appear like a dream – where the back door's open.
I open my mouth to greet you in surprise.
You smile before I've spoken – *Val!*

More suddenly and strangely than any name
You break the spell, telling us all how.

We walk outside, briefly, before we gather
As the sun strikes 8.10 on the clockface.
The light pours over the gravestones
That walk like shadows of the dead ...
The other dead, in stone, that the light is stronger than
As it shadows them and they become bleak thoughts
As I pass them – one by one, black against the light –
Not like birds, *but like nothing that has life,*
Only the shadow that the sun is like gold through.

And in the cave where the crystal sun sets
In the chapel at the back of the house like a crypt, raised
Up a flight of stone steps: there we gather
Under its low tunnel-ceiling, on hard benches,
Sitting in candlelit quiet and then silence, breathing;
Everything about me begins to deepen and loosen ...
As the breath runs down into my arms, legs, feet,
Weighing to sink from heart into belly,
Everything about me becomes a stone, then falls away
As the flow, the darkness opens, and he can let go now.

Take this last part of me that separates me from You

My heart becomes a stone and falls

                                 my bones fall,
My mind falls, voided completely –
And I'm left in the dark, empty and waiting ...

Now we walk out to the pub round the corner
With its fruit-machine lights and dartboard heart,
And I savour the dark liquid with its head of sweet froth
Like a sun in the dark, warming into deep blood-fire
A deep gladness and longing through the whole of my body

As I take your arm, and we walk towards the river
Round the back of the cathedral where the path leads,
Bats flitting around us, and past – overhead
Their black velvet wings skirting soundlessly
As we come down the garden steps on to the Faery Bridge
Spanning the river with its delicate railings

We stand gazing down into the dark
At the water sliding in rapid patterns over the rock,
A smooth shelf of rock, gleaming, raised to the surface.
I gaze at the rock –
                              it is the bedrock

It is the bedrock flooded and brought to flow
As I lean over, drawn down through my eyes,
Mesmerised by its eddying, deliquescent roar –
Brought down to crouch on my heels,
Hanging on to the railings with both hands.
I want to lie down there; I want to lie on the rock,
Lie naked on the bedrock, letting the water flow round me
And over my white body, all over me
As I reach for your hand, silently ...

We talk as we gaze, about desire incarnating
And isn't this the longing? Of spirit becoming matter,
To feel completely into the body of things.
Everything: root, snail, stone, flower, and flesh.
And as you feel it you say it is an ancient longing,
Far away the oldest longing in all of us.

You turn, and suddenly mouth to mouth
We become the river turning in our mouths as we breathe,
We become the river drowning in our ears, flowing under
Eyes, all sense, plunging into its roar, its black streaming,
Until you come up for air, faint with the strength of it,
Half-lying back, dizzy ... We rest apart

With what we have done in wordless freedom
Not even as lovers, but as brother and sister,
Needing no one to believe it,
That it's right now
               for now

In the holy, unholy dark – in the wonder of it –
Streaming around us in the water

To slip down into another skin …
So that I am the light, I *am* the river,
I am the ground I'm walking on,
And then I am compassion …

As we stand slowly, full of what we've shared,
And walk back in silence among the roses,
Their white blossoms glowing, sweet with dew
On your fingertips when you touch them,
On my nose and mouth as I bend to them.

As we walk back under the arch
You lean back to look up at the stars,
The spire of the cathedral lit up ahead,
Its windows blazing like a lit barn,
The floodlighting shadowing the graves,
Gold through the shadow, come through

And as we sit by a stone before coming in,
On a bench as if in ordinary daylight, at midnight,
I see this is what it means to no longer be alone:
No longer needing the wrench of saying goodbye
When from moment to moment we are with what is –
With you, and 'you' everywhere, in any stone,
And it's only then we can be truly alone,
When we're not wanting something or someone else;
I am alone – we are alone – and then we are at one.

Dunblane and the Dorn Path

Light over the graveyard outside,
       Gleaming on the mown grass and the stones
       Set in place, blending back, warm –
The whole morning air as if cleansed
Under the cloudless blue reaching beyond the roof ...
As I imagine walking through them breathing the clear air,
The light's cutting edge like a silent knife;
It is a true light morning to decide in.

I've surfaced, leaving the night behind.
I have surfaced, and the depth is clear.
Only tell me about the man in his animal skin
And how he can wear a skin of light,
A skin that is his own, and Yours ...
Show me the shaman-Christ.

As we leave the chapel on this heaven-sent day
You stand quietly in your heart like Magdalene,
Brought back to your heart inside, as I am to mine,
Our eyes meeting blue and brown in the silence
That the light surrounds, like the sky, without shame
The way You hold us in the truth to ourselves
That waking brings us to, veil after veil
That only means we have further to walk,
Further to go into the Dawn of You

– and we choose to take the Dorn Path on our own.
'See you later, maybe.' 'Enjoy your day!'
Leaving you to your freedom to wander, taking ours,
Leaving the cathedral behind over our shoulders
And walking down the main street, the stores opening,

Past the bookshop you linger at … down to the roundabout
Where the traffic circles and divides at its edges –
Crossing the dual carriageway at a run, for the country,
For a road that came before we knew how to speed.

We climb a stile at its beginning, by a gate
Where it reaches past the outskirts' council houses
Sandpit-bright as toys with children's voices,
Bordering the manicured edge of a golf course, and you say,
'We've returned to reality,' thinking of your own –
Or 'It's a question of shifting levels',
I say to you as we fall into step,
And then, on the ground, there among the pebbles
I see it gleaming … a white stone
 – a white quartz stone, reminding me, *purity* –
And I walk ahead for a moment in silence …

When I turn and wait for you, the tree tells me,
This lime tree with its honeysuckle-like blossoms
Beneath which we meet, gazing up
Into the sheer soft white-blue rising above it,
Its scent of green sticky as its leaves
Filled with light and substance, and you breathe
A kind of relief, as I do, where heaven and earth meet
And we don't even have to say it, it's given
Like the stone into the palm of our eyes.

Sheep grazing among the oaks,
In the silence beyond the traffic roar … thickening,
The cars fall away to the lightest of breezes
Whispering in the air, and the quickening birdsong,
Before we glimpse the vertical, for a moment,
Vaulting up above the rosebay willowherb and grasses
In a gap of blue between two sheer-sided pines –
And it's that leap into silent wonder,
Into the whole height of the Risen World – joy!

Joy, as you feel it in your heart,
Risen beyond it, and into it

                                        you know?

How could you forget?

Then a stark dead tree
By a rainbow-swathe of white cloud descending –
In the bull field with its nettles and thistles …
We look for where he is, in all that edgy space,
Over the empty brow – until we find him
Directly ahead, near the fence, mounting her –
With a thrust of his heavy-sided groaning horn;
Then as we pass him, as if on tiptoe to his privacy,
He sidles up almost shyly against her, seeing us,
I'm sure of it! – as you breathe, touched, amazed –
Brother Bully with his brown eyes and snout

And how could you say he doesn't know either?

The path dipping down among the trees
Past pines, beeches, larches, then an ash by a low wall –
A boundary wall bordering their untrodden depth
Where I sit for a moment to change films,
Rewinding and unwinding the spool,
And suddenly you appear out of nowhere, Tom,
Out of the sunlight like a wandering knight
Who's walked on without his horse –
Or like any traveller, but not of this time,
Your clothes blending out of the trees
And the only real thing is the sunlight on your face
As you bend, surprised, to greet us, 'How do?'

Holding your quiet space, as we hold ours
Following on after you, after a moment or two out of sight:
The river-sound closening down among the trees
As we cross a slatted bridge over a stream tributary

Whose water gleams brown among the leaves
As it weaves its way among wet and dry stones;

And there is the Black Man's Cave
Under a lip of stone like a sideways mouth
Fringed with ferns and bracken, thick green moss
Lining the stones inside like damp cool velvet –
The musky wet smell as we enter and crouch
And have to stoop under the earth-root ceiling,
One at a time, into this wet womb ...
Crouching as we did in the beginning
(As we did last night, as it echoes back)
And because it's the most natural thing to do.

Black man, who were you? The first in Scotland?
Or are you black because you are what we are
That we've left behind, out of the sunlight,
Burying and disowning you under our skins?
Your gift this contradiction
That is no contradiction
As you say *this is the womb you're born from*
And the earth where you will return
Like any fox who knows it's hounded,
Like any mother who knows her bedrock ...

And into this pilgrim wood, where legions have trodden
In the fading gold of their helmets and greaves ...
In this haunted air where everything is alive, and simultaneous,
And as silent as the sunlight glinting in colour
For a moment as you think of them.

We come out where the wild grasses cluster in a field
Blending dry corn and green, islanding two giant hogweed –
And the Allan flows ahead, almost from our feet
Over a dry shelf of rock lined like frozen tide-sand ...
Glinting light and deeper tan-brown in the sun.

As the path climbs up, back among the trees
The water threads beneath through the dappled shade,
We come to a tree with one protruding branch
Reaching out like an arm, with a hollow behind it:
And at its base a stone – a stone that's split –
And where the rock has split you lean back into it,
You lean back in its arms with the stream-flow below
Where you catch a glimpse of Tom's white head in the shadow ...

And I lean back, I lie here, melting
With my head right back and my mind split open,
Split like the stone, until I feel my body shaking,
Gently quivering from throat to feet
As I disappear into the other side of the tree.
'What's the shaking?' I ask you as we stand.
'It's what you get just before flying,' you say,
Meaning when you meditate (TM), as I shake out my arms ...
And we walk on while I think of wings.

We walk on, *part* of the trees now
(And that was the gift of the stone to me),
And glancing down into a clearing we see them,
Hear their voices, over on the other bank –
The boy swinging
                    on a T-bar above the Lady's Pool
– where the vicar's daughter drowned in 1832 –
Shouting as he calls out and the rope twists ...
The boy
            flying, naked in his boxer shorts
As he swings out round from the bank, as he leaps –

His friend standing back, silently watching him daring,
As we do – unseen – drawn into him,
Into his fearless torso that the sunlight loves
As we love him, as he swings, lost in it ...

We move; he plunges harmlessly behind us
And I think of him, swinging —
And You, as ever, always one step ahead.

We reach the weir, where the water begins to break
And a woman is sitting quietly alone ...
Downstream, where it slides under Allan Bridge,
Where the water finally
                                    gives itself away.

At the Allan Water Café with its dark interior,
Glass-fronted doors, like something out of Vienna,
We order tea and ice cream, and you wander in ...
To join us in the shade. You talk about Bonhoeffer
Dying alone in a concentration camp cell —
And the need to have real spiritual guides, real people
(Like George Appleton, you say) who have suffered
Living the paradoxes through themselves ...
When we ask you about your own Christian past
You look down at the table as if in pain:
'I threw it all in before I became a Quaker ...
I wasn't happy about it, knew something was missing,
So I went into the wilderness, and I'm still there.'
Still there, with the sands blowing around you

And as I look at your taut white face I wonder
Is it self-exile? And dare I ask you — yes I do —
If what you're looking for *He* is looking for in you?
'Yes, but what is God?' you ask me —
And all I know is wholeness, is a circle,
Is the whole of what we are You meant us to be.
You agree: and the truth is we can only experience it
Wherever we are in the silence of ourselves,
That inner silence where we truly live and walk
Where we can only come to each threshold alone:
And who can make the horse drink, then? No one —

Though you say, harking back, 'You know, these orders
Are full of people who've had no experience at all!
They're just not qualified.' *No — and are we?*

What does it take before we are ready?
All we know now is we're ready to leave —
And we leave you with the thread fraying, for the sun,
To return in your own time, as we do in ours.
'See you back' — as you broaden into a brief smile
That the sunlight carries as it carries you away.

As we climb the path back up into the woods
I glimpse a child — a young girl — through the branches,
Half standing and half squatting on the opposite bank,
Gazing down at her own reflection in the water ...
And you drift back easy as the sunlight,
A whisper in the softening air, Meister Eckhart, as you say,
'The path is pleasant, and joyful, and familiar.'
And it is, you knew — and we can feel it
In each quiet step as we walk, seeing the path as it is

Till we leave it, deciding to fork down to the river,
Down the dry slope, near the tree, and where you paused
To sit with the river that holds the secret ...
You take off your shoes to wade in
Where the water thrills liquid and cool round your toes,
And I follow you, inching out over the slippery stones
Into the light where you laugh and spread your hands for balance;
And as we sit back on the bank, our feet in the river,
Its flow and fluted tone-by-stone song all around us

I bend with my hands and taste You
I feel you, running over feet and ankles
I cup You in my hands, I cover my face with You

And it's You in the river, like You in the rain ...

I still into its brown-gold surface, and I'm seeing
How each element is so completely into itself
It's no longer self-conscious, there's no self-seeing;
Is water aware of its rushing?
Or fire the serenity of its flame? It *is*,
And then no more are we, being our true selves
Sitting here freed, in our own space.

When we stand, we're like monks without a cowl,
Two beings beyond gender and even our names,
Washing the earth off our feet for our shoes,
Cool to the skin as we climb back to the top
With the river-sound still loud in our ears
Rippling in its sense down our legs as we tread,
The river's silence there is no telling
Till we abandon ourselves and become its water.

So we walk with the river now, like the trees,
As it flows downstream through our feet –
And when we climb away, glancing back,
It blazes and glitters through the branches' green
With a froth of silver, a farewell of light:
River, like You, that is dark and light,
Jet and silver, on fire with sunlight.

As we cross the slatted bridge, leaving it,
The sunlight shadows the outline of a long cross
On the nailed boards, angled as if from behind –
Black against the light, as you step lightly across:
To remind us that *the cross is suffering in time*
As the nails are driven in – and my eyes see it
And there's no avoiding it in the days to come
Before we reach the world that can be
Purified as we dream it
                              – is that it?

It is, and its shadow does not speak

As it dissolves behind us into the leafy glade
We return to as we walk this road like roads would have been:
This royal road of earth now, as it was and will be
As I dream it stripped of tarmac, fast lanes and white lines,
Stripped of all we have crucified it with,
As it reverses in time
                         deep in the heart
                         of time

As the trees come back, and lean in close –
So that the rider on the horse
             has to bow under their branches;
Now we bow under the light, silently giving thanks to it
As the sun shadows the length of it under two alley walls
The wild grass grows over in place of wire.

We come through where the wall ends;
The sheep graze and gather under the shadow of a tree
Whose branches reach out to embrace them – so finely etched
They could be under moonlight, that is daylight, sunlight
As in a Samuel Palmer painting they compose,
Its canvas become a dream realer than you could imagine:
The tree, its shadow, the grass, and their soft coats
In this here-now pastoral, where they gaze, their gaze returned
In the soft late light that is turning to gold

As the walls of your house become glass around you ...
And we cross the road, the light walking in us
So that the cars are dreamlike, and the grass is real.
We reach the main street where the shops are closing,
The buildings like a backdrop, and the realest thing
Is you walking beside me, towards me, behind me,
And nothing have we made that doesn't speak of this,

That doesn't say We Are What We Dream
In the higher lucid dream we are being dreamt in.

We come to the west wall of the cathedral
And wander in, hearing the music ...
Vaulting dimly under its high-windowed arches.
We open to the door to it like wind hurrying leaves ...
We tread the threshold over its scratched stone flags
And cross to where the axis hangs at the centre
Up the length and breadth of the aisle, by the choir
While the organist plays, the notes rapid and climbing
As we turn by the pulpit and the carved misericord
And glance up at the blaze of colour in the windows
Overarching, hidden from outside.

So the windows begin: filled by Michael and Gabriel
With their staffs, and their faces like children
 – Uriel and Raphael framing them –
Standing in red and gold, all of one family,
Their faces showing no trace of closure or disdain.
The organ bursts into alto refrain, with the stops out,
As the heavens open: sun, moon, and stars in red-gold –
Clouds, and the four winds in climbing swathed figures
Perfect in their nakedness, newly recreated,
While the angels above open their palms to receive them
Ascending in one continuous ladder of breath.

The notes swell under the vaulted ceiling, louder;
They swirl, spiral, and eddy – as if improvised –
Filling our eyes and blood as we come into Chaos
Like the next stage of the prophecy, that is fire
With its blazing eye of wind, hail, ice, and snow –
As they struggle over the wastes towards the Pole,
Lost in the whiteness, blinded in its naked glare
Like pilgrims reaching to where no skin can reach
But it obliterates all sense – and in the flood of *Now*

That dissolves everything into liquid, naked feeling
Before it can begin again

And now Earth, you come through – Earth, New Earth –
As the organ becomes a stately full march
Layered within itself, simultaneously walking,
With the animals first, then grass and water –
Released like a blessing into the depth of the colours
While the dove hangs hovering above, suspended down,
Infusing every colour, every nuance and shade,
Saying, *'It is of this Light you came'*, yes, by grace,
And by the grace of peace that is bliss –
That is the most natural thing there is,
All form, all face, and all texture – oh feel it!

And then we come last, Humanity – out of this
Reborn in Creation and no longer apart from it –
With Adam and Eve, Jacob and David, and the three
Who sang the Benedicite, and the music becomes chords,
Sustained chords, struggling to rise and crown it
As the blessed make their way into the City of Age
Beyond time, that is pearl outliving life
That all the passion of our lives becomes, substantial;
Here is Blane, and here is William Blake,
In one brotherhood and sisterhood with Margaret
Climbing the stairway of heaven into the sun

As the music ends, on its plateau, and we breathe down:

'O all ye works of the Lord, bless the Lord'

– and we can ...

We drive north to Peace House at Greenloaning,
To sit on the lawn outside, where we belong –
Spread out on rugs over the moistening grass.

124

We talk about creativity or violence, Helen,
And I see we can't have peace without either –
I mean: not full-blooded peace, or the best is suppressed
And who are we then? We cast a long shadow
Of pastel shades, floating airs, and hypocrisy
That is never what angels were or will be!
You nod, glancing down, before we go inside to eat.

Sitting inside, crammed in – thirty of us
In the front drawing room, on chairs, on the floor –
We talk about our journey and the meaning of pilgrimage
As a faith beyond itself, where we meet in the heart –
Bahai, Buddhist, Hindu, Christian, or Quaker,
'The poetry does not matter' and neither does the name.
Only if I tell you what kind of journey I'm on
And ask you what yours is will you feel it
As a movement within, and then you'll know
That even driving from A to B can be it,
In what we're all secretly moving in …

Then, as you speak his prayer, Margot,
'Lord make me an instrument of thy peace …'
A train outside passes like a great sigh
Echoing down the tracks, somewhere south into sadness;
And outside through the window and over the grass
The light's a thin strip of gold on the horizon
Under the woven grey rising cirrus cloud
As we sit in silence, and our breathing holds,
A tractor is passing, everything is passing,
Two dogs are barking, the swifts are flitting and circling
In the dove-grey air, in the gathering twilight:

'Shantih, shantih, shantih'

Give our souls peace.

Western Argyll – Loch Awe

We do not know how to pray as we ought
But the Holy Spirit intercedes for us;
We do not know how to pray as we ought
But the Holy Spirit intercedes for us
With sighs too deep for words …

As we sit in the chapel, on this blue morning
Together before your leaving, Dorothy, and ours;

And as you speak the prayer it hangs in the silence
On the other side of blueness, that is your sadness,
The grief you'd never shared till these last moments
When it churns in the upset stomach you woke with,
Shadowing your eyes in your shades.

Bread of Christ, Body of Christ,
Your frozen shoulder and your numb tongue,
Christ in the Garden, Christ in the Silence,
And the body of us you lean on invisibly
'With sighs too deep for words …'
And the shadow of the cross in your eyes.

You're a bubble of suffering surrounded by the blue,
One who has to go into the dark when it's all bright,
And in your aloneness all I can meet you with is *eyes* –
Words won't do, and I don't know you,
But the bread that breaks is pure feeling
When you show us the parts we can always deny,
Reminding us that endings are not neat and tidy
But ragged, loose, and raw as they are if they're real;
Only then can they be beginnings, too …

And your gift in leaving us is onwards into soul,
The shadow you hold for us bursting like fruit
Even in your tears that wouldn't fall. Ours, too.
So I thank you.

The luggage piled on the pavement while we fuss in English
About where to put things, and you come back from the station;
We stand around waiting, and I check the map,
Kneeling down to one side, for the Loch Awe route.
I want to take you to a sacred place I know
Where the peace glows down like rain and the body breathes open.

I want to take you to a garden
Where love has never ended
And the dead have buried their dead in wild flowers.

We motor out like a hearse for the living
Echoing the sky, leaving the Cathedral Square behind us
As we go down through the town and branch out west ...
Towards Doune, Callander, and the Highlands,
The green transparency
                           rising as I drive
Through open country – to the Pass of Leny
Where the lochs split the land
                              in blue strips, like scars,
Wounds of sky from under the ground

And nothing breaks the blueness the Land is Risen in,
Standing under the sky, expanding into itself,
Vaulting above the pines either side of the road
As we pass Loch Lubnaig into Strathyre Forest

And the names become water, earth, and air
Elementally themselves under the fire of the sun
Transformed into light, and the light into blue horizon.

We pause by a garden centre,
Sit at white tables under greenhouse glass,
Drinking tea, the scent of plants and soil all around us.
I go outside to find a place to pee before we leave,
And I come to a gap in the trees … pathlike, it stretches
Narrow along their border, mown through wild grass –
A narrow path that leads the whole way to the mountain,
Reaching ahead beyond the telephone wire and poles
To where it rises, with no space to stray left or right
And no space for more than one alone.

As I drive us on in silence, and the silence it brings
Reaches into my eyes and the roof of my mouth,
The phrase comes as I listen within its hearing:

'Mouth of silence,
Womb in which the Word can form …'

I taste it in my mouth; I taste the silence
And the space inside it, thick and slow on my tongue
In a longing to speak, and speak authentically.

We pass Loch Earn … and the land opens
Into a further emptiness
                              past Ben More and Ben Cheathaich,
Their sheer sides empty even of sheep

– driving rhythmically, at one with the road –

An austere land, in which even the mountains
Are almost indifferent to the forest planted on them
As they soar above, to the height of eagles,
And we observe them, as they do us
From the air above their heads
As if to say

'This is our strength
	grounded in dominion'

As we enter Glen Lochy, under the eye of You
Where there is space, and more space, for You

Lord of the Silence
That is the truth in ourselves

Whatever that truth can bring
			and shall

With twenty miles to go, or less,
Before the loch dips down like a streaming torrent,
We stop at a hotel to hide inside for lunch,
Walking the gravel path, as you paced it, the words in your ears,
Your form become invisible, on the other side of silence
A flickering grey shadow with the mountains and the rain.

In this sun: emptiness, everything evaporates
As the page opens like the present to what is here now
And what is waiting, suspended, to come into being ...
The road leads down like a flickering tongue of sunlight
To Kilchurn – on its faery islet
Beyond the trees where I point to its hollow shell
That only the wind is fit to blow through –
And you join me within, where we were, again
Finer than sunlight, invisibly inside me
Spreading out through my eyes over the water.

Where the road reaches inland, down to Cladich
With its river bridge and lion-tongue of tan water ...
You catch sight of the shaggy Highland heifer
Standing under an oak, above us, and we stop:
Superb, long-horned, four-square in his russet coat,
Regal, deer-weighted, his immovable gaze

Staring back from the other side of the wire.
'Oh,' you say, Eileen, 'he's posing!'
He doesn't even need to blink to reply *stupid*
As the whole earth shores to stillness under his feet.

We come down to the church we always passed
With its grey walls and slate like mercury in the light.
This time we pull over to go in ... I skirt
Its narrow green-gated metal porch to glance up
At the belfry with its tuft of weed sprouting at the top.
I follow you into the aroma of flowers
Within this church for the living
Where you sit among the pews, I *see* her,
Or sense her before I see her, in the stained glass
Holding her child like a queen, he sitting freely
Above the hem of her skirt glowing red like a rose ...

Rose, and the scent is rose as we sit
Cloaked in its stillness, and then enfolded in it,
And as I breathe I inhale you like a rose;
You warm across my chest and my heart opens
As we sit in the Rose, all of us, in it ...
I open my eyes, and they adjust in the glow,
Seeing the flowers filling bowls, bunched by the altar step,
Pale pink, white, red, ruby, and primrose yellow
With a single red bloom by the pulpit. As we stand
I breathe it into my heart and the warmth there
That no sun alone can bring, where the sign says OPEN.

You close the gate quietly behind you, John,
Your hand shaking and your eyes looking down
As you all stand around in the sunlight: Val, Rosemary,
Your eyes open, smiling, unspokenly touched
By the truth of the silence that is the Rose at the heart

                        as we laugh, easy.

'It's a church the women have got into,' as you put it, Val –

And we drive on, glimpsing the loch through the trees,
Transformed out of its rain-grey silver
Into this deep navy sea-blue in the Summerland light,
With the green of its trees, bracken, ferns, grasses,
All the shades of green gathered in the light –
And a copper beech blazing, leaved with light!
The borderland gone, dissolving into memory
As we pass where we camped by Crow Island,
The oval mouth of mud grown over back to grass,
The grass covered with caravans and playing children,
And I flash a smile with my eyes to you south ...

We come to the Falls, and I listen for the water
Hidden off the road, plunging among the trees
Where we climbed, and you hang on to the wire
Where we've pulled in by the gate, squeezing in,
And we cross the sodden field quaked lumpy in the heat,
Cracked and caked among thistles
                    as if the ground has shaken.
We closen to the river and scale the fence,
'And it's like this, you have to work for wildness,'
I tease you when it's half between your legs ...
Then you shame us completely as we sit and watch
While you roll up your trousers and wade right in, Maeve,
With Eileen in tow, into the freezing white water.
'It's lovely!' you shriek. 'Won't you join us?'
As Tom sits demurely unpeeling his socks
And John stands back intoning *I don't think so*
You dabble among the icy pebbles with your toes ...

Then as we leave on the road past Innis Chonel
The castle gives way to a tiny pine tree island
Above the road, a tiny single white cloud

The size of innocence beyond experience, and ours.
Which comes first, then? Which comes last?

I feel the border of silence closening,
The stalking border, where I need to be silent
As we deepen among the Eredine trees and the sunlight
Flakes in pools of brightness in their evergreen shadow.

I want you to feel this place for yourselves,
So I switch the engine off and we glide
Lightly downhill with the breeze in the leaves
And the sound of the water lapping beyond them,
Just the leaf and water sound, not our voices
But theirs, now … as you closen to your silence
And the spell of the air hangs, if you want it to –

The engine spurts back into life, for the last bend
Before we reach the fishermen's lay-by, and reverse in,
And I ask you all for silence.

Here's where we walk. Here's where it is.

The track ascending, with its wheel ruts, as you follow
And the pine scent drifts, lacing the air
As I bow my head and climb, breathing it in,
Asking for silence in myself

And the path like a dream, so familiar,
A lucid dream where I've been walking ever since
Dreaming myself, *him*, back to the wire gate
Where he climbs above himself now to earth and sky
And stands looking at you, Kilneuair: your walls
Broken and intact, waist high through the bracken,
And I trace an encircled cross over my chest
As a supplication, permission to enter:

I cross the threshold, and wade
Where the breath hangs in the sunlight and the green
And there's no sound, only the breath whispering,
Humming inaudibly like bees, at my feet.

Stop, look again, listen:
Everything, the stones, graves, flowers, is so clear
It's as if through crystal, like perfect vision
So clear and awake you can't believe you're not dreaming,
When you're more than awake!

And the light pours down, the light is pouring down
Over my head, drawing me into silence
So there's no difference between the light
And what it's shining on – it's all one place
And I have no name, I am a thing of the light,
A person and a creature of the light,
And I am nothing about myself I recognise
But myself as I am, with these hands and eyes.

I see you walking, shadowed against the light
In the colours of your clothes as you wander apart
With only the sound of your feet, and no word –
No word for what we become here, not yet
While I stand by the font, then sit on the low wall,
And as I close my eyes I lose you

I let you all go

And the light is pouring down into my head,
Down my arms, into my thighs and feet.
The light is my heart and my eyes.
The light is peace, dazzling, radiant soft peace
In the veins of my hands and my blood now
Raining down behind my eyes, pressing me still,

Speechless, immovable and still — as I lean
With the warm stone under, holding me, and you say

Be at peace. Your task now is to learn peace.
Know the peace of the ground, of the light come down.
The holy ground is peace, and the ground words come from
Is silence, is this ... and from silence to peace, feel life
And know this is the Light Come Down you saw
On that city bridge: feel what it means here
In the breeze in the trees, the sound of the flies,
The birds, bees, and the warmth of the wall beneath.

Peace, my son. Be at peace.

Peace the source from which all you speak will come
And all you will be will come. In peace you find Me.

All the lightness and all the beauty there ever is
Come from peace and return to peace
And underneath both of them is peace, and the Beginning.

I reach for the recorder, and it is still.
Everything's still. I open my eyes, you've gone,
And I could have been here for hours, for a life.
You've come from the other side to find me,
Infusing me with your energy — brother, lover, guide.
You echo in my mind — peace —
And as I gaze up everything speaks you
And it's still speaking, in the flowers, the leaves
As the light spills off them, and is always speaking,
Always here, only we have gone ...

I stand slowly and give thanks
Out towards the mountains over the loch
Where their edges blend with the rim of the sky.
I start to walk back, the light and the peace

Reaching under my feet into the ground.
I glance back as I round the walls, go through the gate,
Until they disappear under the bracken and trees:
And nothing seems simpler than this, or more complete.

It's an open secret I cannot hold or speak.

But when I come down you've been waiting;
You meet me with impatience and irritation
I can see in your eyes, although nothing's said.
I'm crushed back into my being in the driver's seat.
'We had a misunderstanding about time,' you offer
As an olive branch; and I'm sad and that's that.
Even when you thank me, and I don't need thanks,
You bring me to the fiery ache of what I am.

Can you be open like the day?
Where the light holds and the peace remains
And is that the test of it? I fail, then I make it,
Winding the window down to let in the breeze,
Letting it go, and loving you as you are, as it is,

As the light spreads everywhere

                    vivid on the green, silently

And over the last of the waters of Loch Awe
As we reach its end and turn to go north again –

My heart stripped silently of pride and pain,
Quietly while I feel you breathing at my back
And I gaze out beyond myself again
                              with you now
As we descend . . .

Your Country, lit up by the billion-watt candle of Your Sun

And the sea!
                    We round the edge of it, above

          its white breakers cresting in from Shuna ...

And on the shores of Loch Melfort the sea fills in;
On a long narrow strip of stone beach, a horse
With the light blazing on the water in front of his bowed mane,
The horse!
                    Rebirth, as you said

– weathered in the heart, and beaten gold
Born in the heart that can see him and exult.

When you ask about Druidry, I tell you what I know:
That a priest of light meets a priest of earth
In the heart of an oak, where he stands his ground,
And you listen with your doubting academic mind
As the land soars around us like an open-hearted storm
And I wonder about yours, in the blush of your cheeks
As you fall silent, Rosemary, looking out to sea ...
And the road reaches inland;
                              as we come down to Oban

Kilneuair fades behind us like a dream

                    or the gateway to another dream.

We thread through the streets to the Royal Hotel
Huge above its glass swing doors, like pseudo-London,
Its endless rooms down endless red corridors ...
We take our keys vanishing up into the labyrinth:
And the Love Hotel is facing out to sea
With its endless stream of anonymous souls,
One night stands, and late night taxis
And we are in the Hotel World yet not of it

136

As we border the sea among the wheeling cry of gulls
To a very different destination;

Opening the window, five storeys up,
Looking out over the roofline at a blunted turret
Above the pile of windows and the garrets next door,
I catch a glimpse beyond, of a spire on the horizon
Under the brightening white cloud, just out to sea
And almost out of sight as it blends with the white of it ...

We gather downstairs to eat,
The dining hall like a vast inflated B&B
With its laid-out tables, two-choice menu, and trolleys,
Families, kids, faces of all shapes and sizes –
Expanding to Humanity.

In the bar afterwards near the front of house
You sidle up smiling, Margot, and ask what I'd like,
Then you sit conspiratorially, saying,
'Don't cast pearls before swine, you know?'
Tempted to agree, I wrestle inside
(With a phrase I've never fully understood):
But we're not swine, Margot; it's too late for that now.
Or what did you mean? Wisdom, like a snake,
Smiling back at me with your older, knowing eyes,
Tempter and friend, as you add, 'or it's wasted.'
I don't know the answer; I only know the dream:

All I know is I want to take you off this page
Into the thing itself, that is yours, in you.
All I know is, if we could trust the silence,
We could know what to do and break every schedule,
Living in the inner freedom of our truth
Even while the world breaks around us like clockwork.

Am I dreaming, or is the light turning gold outside
As it slants over the façade of the buildings?
And it's still this: *Do you believe in the sunlight,*
Or is the sunlight only sunlight in your eyes?

We wander the late streets, to the esplanade and sea-edge
Where the salt smell wafts towards us on the air
With the gulls, their white bellies and wings in the twilight
— the salt smell of harbours, of Piraeus and Santorini —
Till the ship's horn brings the sunrise, and she comes ...
'We are leaving for islands', and we are leaving again,
Standing facing Mull across the darkening stretch,
The water like dyed blue silk in the light

As we watch a fishing smack inching in ...
Red and white prow, mast lights, a gull flying round it
Lit up by the floodlights arcing out.

We walk on past the boys on the esplanade
Waiting around in groups — by a car — on the sea wall,
Eating cooling bags of chips as they pace
Waiting for something to happen. It's like a movie track,
But what happens doesn't happen next.
Nothing happens, and they wait in the gaps.
For Christ's sake is anything ever going to happen
And is it a rose, a revving gear change, or a knife?

We pass through to walk on the quiet side
Round where the railings reach beyond the street lamps.
You talk about opening a new space in your life
And how that's initially exclusive — it's *you.*
As you sit on the pavement and take off your shoes
Then carry them, barefoot, and your step changes
I tell you I've always seen you as your own person.
And here she is — I watch you, walking alone,

Glancing down as we remember the moment we met,
And how we're given to each other *to become ourselves* ...

The light over the water darkening into blue-black,
Mull withdrawn into an outline of shadow,
Only the fishing lights winking like sea-stars
Come close and bright

Like messengers from another world, and ours,
Across the great divide, as the air hangs still.

Day 15

Oban – Mull

Hung over with the simmering grey heat of the night,
Tossing and turning in its grey choking blanket
Of smoke I inhale as I open the window and lean out –
But no respite, till the dawn breaks white within it
Like a cool outbreath of air ...
I've lain awake, as you have, making the dawn come
To disturb this chrysalis shell.

Held in tiredness and reverie. It's right.
I'm as soft as the day breaking over my head ...

Walking out on the morning streets
At half speed, to catch the post to you –
As I cross the road where a green van is unloading,
The road rising into the circle of the amphitheatre above,
Beyond an old man in mid-step on the white line with his stick;
I glimpse the circle with its tall hollow windows of air
Encircling it all, and the town like a crown.

It will be whole ...
                    The postcard leaves my hand
And I'm walking along, laden, to the ferry harbour,
Rounding the quiet street as I imagine it reaching you,
Its ink dried in mist, stamped, blackened, trodden,
As the sea opens out, stained with slicks of oil.
The gulls hover there, and it mirrors them, wing for wing
As they half-land and perch seeking scraps of anything.
Watching their hunger dance from the jetty,
The passengers gather, drifting out from the barrier,
Standing around, watching, waiting in the sunlight,
Gazing out to where the esplanade buildings are still.

Out of all that expanse, it comes: Caledonian MacBrayne.
Like an ark, a Ship of God, a box high out of the water,
It skirts at its own pace, like something inevitable,
Like You out of the void the emptiness ends in –
As we breathe and, like sleepers, start to move
Long before it's in, reaching for baggage, as if
It had somehow vanished in our gazing: the ballast, the weight.
We are creatures of gravity, so we lumber.
We are creatures of fear, and so we linger.
Lord, help us to let go!

We herd the gangplank in a line, divided in queues,
Spreading up to the top deck, quickening for places
Around the foghorn, on benches, on the green metal floor –
Then we wait as it moves, imperceptibly breathing,
Before the engines thunder and flood.
We sail at noon.

And as we move, reversing and turning,
The prow easing round towards a gap in the headland,
I breathe over the sea, leaning over the railing,
And the breeze hits my face, the gulls gathering behind,
The water sliding beneath towards the open sky;
I'm being cut loose from my feet – as it rises
Into my throat – my eyes – and my mind

With the Highlands gone behind
                                        and the road, the path
A scur of back-foam stretching in its wake ...

We pass the castle blended with ivy and trees,
Heading out towards the open sea

The mainland etched already distant in the heat-mist
Shimmering in the light that veils it
                                        like Venice.

The gulls come close, flying
with the white of their wings above the foam

And the light of this breath of the sea rising in me,
An inner light rising up my spine to meet it,
Awakening my whole body through my eyes –
The light song rising not in words, but light,
As light to light through my open mouth
Rising to sing above the hum of the ship's engine
As if I could sing and always be singing

And in singing, draw earth, air, and sky
Into me as light as I praise it, breathing light
As all its energy and mine streams as light
In the streaming the song becomes, and is

As you join me at the railing and we glance down
Over the fringe of moving foam
                              at the atoll of Maiden Isle

– where the virgin lives,
The woman who is invisibly one-in-herself –

                    rising in its bare mound

              with the white sail of a yacht

              like a triangle beside it

As a gull flies and hovers, feet above, like the song,
Its white spread in the soft white explosion of cloud
Raying out around in brush-streaks of cirrus –
So close you could reach up to it like a dove ...

We sit back on the bench, quietly in meditation,
The deck vibrating under our feet,

And I open my eyes still wider awake

in the dream

We could be sailing on the roof of the world
Floating above, on the green globe of the deck
With the sky's high cirrus like a crown above us

our crown and source

as we breathe it in

From the vastness of where we come from, and are
On the edge of this world where the real world waits
And interpenetrates every visible thing it is

as the song says

as the breath says

And everything we do that breaks through is seeing
This Song of our hearts, eyes, and being that is silence
That sees and knows — as you breathe awake, smiling
And in no one else's but your own ...

The tannoy breaks in with its information
From its red wall, crackling behind us.
The captain speaks, as if we were in flight

On the roof of the world that is sea, air, and neither —
As we gaze out to the white phallus

of the lighthouse

on Lismore Island

— and the forty minutes trickle by like sand —

And in front of the wall, as the tannoy rasps shut,
Leaning up against it by the unlit strip lighting
Two women sit, their eyes closed, like an androgyne
On the right with her long hair and cap reversed,
The other with crew-cut hennaed hair and
Her arms on her knees, as we sway gently; they sit still
Softened by the sun somewhere far inside
Where two women make two lovers that are one,
Two lovers, or friends, like the moon and the sun.

Mull looms ahead like a ghost in the mist,
A ghost of mountain in the greying white air of the sea.
In the haze of the white its upper curve rises under
As it slowly becomes green, shoreline and detail,
And the mass of its gateway greets us with silence:

                like a punctuation

Landing by inches; before the boat opens its bowels
For the cars to creep out and bump up the ramp.
As the dizzy air grounds
              with their docking growl

We queue to go out and down
Cloaked into matter …

And while you bring the minibus round we re-gather
To go inland from Craignure, into the island's rugged emptiness
Where the houses fall away to its green in minutes

        its grey-green expanse of rain and mountains.

We loop south from Torosay
                into its Empty Quarter

Its dunes piled into green, silence, and shale,
Its green Sahara of Silence silencing us

As we follow the one road through, the only way there is,
The one they used to walk, the old pilgrim route
We glide over in tarmac as I think of them
Travelling to see Columba down the centuries ...
It's just too easy, this driving around.
It's too fast; the distance is suddenly *too soon*.
The spirit of the journey says, as I say it to you,
We need to get out and walk ... and then we say so

As the road winds into Glen More

       and we follow the beige coach ahead

As tiny as a dinky toy
       dwarfed by these mountains

Submerged, and risen
       buried, and rising

Like a sea in front of our eyes, on both sides ...

     Sgurr Dearg, Ben Buie, Beinn Talaidh, Corra-bheinn

We check the map to see how far it is ...

Then the moment comes, in the middle of nowhere:
'Here's fine ... no really, this will do ...'
We slow to stop and get out and leave you
With no one else around – and you wave us away
Abandoned to silence as you fade up ahead out of earshot
In a mid-afternoon siesta without end
Where the only reference point is a postbox!
You stand by it, scanning its collection times,

With your rucksack and walking stick for a staff,
Before we turn and face the silence together
And we breathe in … *'Ah, that's better'* …
Now all we have to do is walk and walk and walk ahead

Following the road to the end. As it rises
We pause for a moment: nothing moves, nothing is,
Only the land breathing back, as our minds empty.
We walk where there's only the green and the stone,
Where no one has built and no one has ploughed.
Every detail stands out as our eyes rove for something;
A ruined croft high out of reach on a hillside,
So broken to the wind you can barely see it.
Now we come to a stream by the side of the road,
Two shockingly blue butterflies parting so quickly
They might never have been seen against the blue
Of the sky they vanish into like a dream …

I sit in the long grass, among the buttercups
Tall and wild on their stems, spangled yellow.
I cup my hands to the soft rain-taste of the water
That is the blood of the stone and the breeze.

Cleanse us, empty us, purify us, ripen us

I wash the whole eye of my face clean.

We round the corner into Bunessan
With its handful of houses reaching round to the sea;
Decide to stop briefly at the café,
The last oasis before the farthest shore …

We sit at a chequered Cream Tea table, waiting
While you evaluate postcards to send.
A man squeezes behind me to get back to his place,
Smiling as I turn: 'Sorry, it's a narrow passage!'

In his mannered French voice. I smile at the metaphor
And noticing the book under his arm I ask him,
'What are you reading there?' It's a book on Gaelic.
As I blink in disbelief he nods at us;
He says again, 'It's a difficult path;
I don't know if I'll get to the end' – like a messenger.

The young waitress smiles as we pay her,
Then puts on her helmet and whizzes off
On her moped outside into the air of her freedom.
I'm wondering where she goes and what she does,
For the road outside shows no trace of her either way,
Only grey gravel-tarmac and dust ...

We follow it rounding the bay in a matter of yards
Before the emptiness begins again.
I glance down at a shape floating in the water
And it is death, my heart sinks, among the weeds,
Is it a swan? It is impossible to tell
 – it isn't near enough to see – but is the swan dead?
The swan song? Has loneliness died? Has love?
Beside it is life: a few feet further on
Where a late lamb is suckling from its mother on a rock,
Pulling at her teats, as white as it, under her ...
And between them, beyond them, you notice him first,
Motioning me to slow down
                              quieten and hush

Is the heron; standing gaunt, blended in grey
So nearly invisible we could have missed him –
On a rock, by the water's edge, poised above the shallows,
Standing on his thin legs with his coat of feathers ruffling
In the breeze, and he stands stock still
As we breathe, expecting him to move, and he stays
While the shallows move like underwater heather and hay
Floating as he waits, knowing his time:

Bird of death and life,
He raises his neck as if listening, twisting his head up
To a sound beyond sound, carried from the sea …
From a mind we cannot think in and only he can reach
As it reaches him – as he brings his head round
And looking down with a movement of his whole body
Brings one webbed foot forward, then the other –
And then his razor-sharp sleek bill stabbing down, down
One, as quick as a knife in the water, and he swallows

And then draws his neck in, to stand again
As he turns slightly, the air ruffling his front plumage
As if he can hear the slightest movement of the water
The backwash of a fishing boat covers, while he waits
Hunching back suddenly like a little old priest
Until it passes – then he moves again
His orange-lined beak parts like well-practised scissors
As if to speak, and brings his neck back up
As if miles away, among the mountains and the cloud

Then with a sudden lunge – out of nowhere –
His beak goes back into a square inch of water
In a flash like lightning far faster than your finger
On the shutter where all our seeing dissolves …

Leaving him, with his lunar neck like silver,
Snake-silver, in a shimmering like light that isn't sun,
Or grey-shot cloud, or white invisible expanse –
There is only his presence, until he decides to leave,
Abruptly
            lifting his wings and flapping away

With his feet left dangling: his wings pterodactyl
As he disappears among a thicket of beech –
Leaving the shore like a mirror to gaze in.

What do you see in the grey of your own face?
'I see it dissolving into rock and water.'
And what do you see then?
'I see the water and the rock
Dissolving into a sky that is my breathing ...'
And what do you see then?
'I see nothing, and everything is breathing;
I have seen the beginning and I have seen the end.'

We walk on slowly round the corner;
Now the air hangs grey with the sky of him, like him ...

We come downhill where the sea spreads out
To the edge of the loch and the island's rim,
Walking apart in our own space. I reach ahead and
Glance down to the moored boats in the natural harbour,
Bobbing on the swell, and the gulls at their lunch hour,
Resting on the water, on the lazy horizontal
Where the whole space hangs relaxed, as we need it to be
In heron-time ... and with time to breathe.

We round uphill again near a ruined croft
We leave the road to wander over to, and find two sheep
Asleep together by the far wall. We walk quietly away
As they graze in stillness with their black faces and horns
Among the bracken, past a black and white marker post
Leaning, scarred by the weather and the rain.

Feeling the heat under our feet
On the hard relentless tarmac in the afternoon's low,
We tread in the rhythm of a silent inner dream,
Too tired to talk, as if we could walk like this for ever,
Never reaching the end with nowhere to rest.
'And it's like that, sometimes you just have to keep going,'
Your voice drifts back into mind,

And who knows what the silence is secretly forging
With each coagulate step ...?

We raise our heads by the side of a house
Where the washing is hanging, billowing in the breeze
Like flags, party flags, yellow, blue, and red,
A sudden spurt of colour like a promise
As they catch our eyes and our steps lighten;

And on the other side, where you look for cover
In all the space around us where there's none
And I stand guard on the road's edge,
You squat to the rush of your blood in the grasses
Where the sheep graze ... and you leave it there
Like a woman from centuries before
As your face clears and your eyes deepen
And as we walk on I feel the blood in you of Woman
With the tang of its after-scent lacing the air.

We leave the road for the rutted edging beside it
Where the earth has dried, like a green pavement
Broadening in and out of single file –

Until we come to the side of an immaculate wall,
Dry-stone built of boulders, perfectly aligned
Where the gaps of field and sky show through ...
Glimpsing the Stone on the other side in the grass,
Standing nine feet high like a softened blade,
We cross through the gate where a woman's sons
Are walking in to plant potatoes. They greet us,
Reassure us it's fine to be walking here,
And you turn and recognise Andre from the café
Waiting silently by the verge ...

You stand by the Stone, and I leave you space
There among the long grasses on your own.

I recognise you, woman in time, with your bare arms
— sweater tied loosely round your waist —
Knowing how to touch it like a lover
As the breeze whispers back through your hair
And the knot at your waist sags like an unborn child.

I stand, clearing the waist-high nettles,
Feeling the pink and white quartz surface with my palm.
When I close my eyes I can remember it too —
And it's healing stone, warm stone, like an embrace
Covered over with dry lichen on the facing side.
It says *healing, you are for healing now*,
Reaching out its armless arms and heart,
Its unarmed, disarmed heart in mine.

As we come out, the messenger is waiting to go in,
His moped parked, his guidebook to hand.
We scan the map where there is no map —
'Only the territory', as you put it,
Beyond the borderland where there is only presence
And names and reasons fall away to touch and being:

This is the emptiness, that it gives us space to feel in
Beyond ourselves, without props or distractions —
So that the edges of who we are begin where we end,
Travelling out to the furthest edge of the sky …
And in the emptiness it sinks, it settles in
So that heron becomes heron and stone becomes stone
In all their after-resonance within us

Till I'm glad of the emptiness, where there's only sheep
And still desert, by a garage with its barking dogs,
Dry forecourt, and peeling paint, where it's Mull-Mexico
As we closen to the last long final flat stretch …

The road reaching straight towards a white house

I'm looking above, into a dark cloud
With a hole at its centre that is becoming the sun
That was and is and is breaking through now,
Raying down as the blackness blinds behind it –
And as it breaks down beyond the tiny islets
And the grey shore's outline lifting beyond them
I can see Iona
                              – it quickens down my spine
And in your eyes as we pause, standing as they stood,
The generations, the sun warming on their faces
And the grey-silver glass of the water the reeds
Are mirrored in, like fine strands of electric hair
Green, tall green and slender, listening:

Oh listen to the wind now
Listen to the Sun
Listen to this moment of seeing

Wherever it ends, it is begun

And so we reach Achaban House, and you ...

In the silence we drive round to Red Bay
With its rugged pink rocks, facing the Island.
While you bow into the cottage door of the restaurant,
I stand gazing across the water to Dun I –
The mountain made for each of us, that all of us can climb:
Dun I, and I am, in the twilight dove-soft haze ...
Dun I, and I can see you and my shadow there ...
Dun I, and all there is, is this waiting
And the stance of waiting that is longing and readiness
To stand as we are, uncounted –

So may I be with You there, and be open
Doing everything I need to be so
Following every prompting, every intuition

152

I give my prayer to the wind and the Dove ...

We go inside and wait around on the sofas,
Come out on the dot of nine, striking ...
And cool, wet, sudden on the back of my hand
The first raindrop falls like a tear from the sky –
Then through the rain mist the Abbey bell is chiming,
Each echo pealing like fading breath ...

Inside where we sit round these long tables
With the brightness of the candles and your laughter
I hear nothing but the Rashputan women you describe
With their grace like goddesses, pots on their heads,
In their best saris – and what are they going to do?
'Put dirt on the road ...' and that's beauty;
It lights up in your eyes, and I see them.
As the light in your eyes reaches my heart
Nothing else stays or holds, the way
The Abbey bell holds the silence that is pure:

There's a silence over the water
And through the rain-mist
You can hear the bells begin to chime ...

I tell you how *outside is inside*, and this?
Is our other island –
Our island of pleasure, jest, and ephemera
And how we belong in both is the mystery.

You speak through it as you reach us, John,
When you say the pilgrimage is lifelong,
It is all our lives, and before, and after –
And it was never less, through the millennia
Or in this moment that has brought us together.
And you say, David, it is letting go;
You evoke the Buddhist monk with his bowl,

With all that emptiness in a circle of brass ...
When you speak of it, Margot, it is Ghandi;
They scattered flowers into the river,
Walking down silently in hundreds after his death;

And it was you, little Krishnamurti,
Standing behind the door when we met,
Not presuming I had come to meet you
(Just holding it open for me to pass through).

The bell chimes on, inaudible in the rain.
It's in these moments 'half-heard between two waves'
That the poetry meets us as we become it – friends,
All of you, all of us in this hush

That is heron, stone, mountain, and Dove.
I hug you without saying it, sister –
As the flame in your heart reddens like the sun.

Day 16

Mull – Red Bay

A steel wire
         slicing sleep from waking –
A steel probe, laced with freezing air,
Throbbing through to a needle point
In the raw drum of my inner ear, as I turn
Awake on the floor, downstairs.

Outside in the wind and the sun-blown grass
I reach up my hand, cupping my palm over it,
Jabbing, searing through a bubble of punctured skin.

I've heard too much, and I need to listen.
The pain points me beyond your voices –
Listen to the silence, into the left stream.

And so You drive me suddenly within …
'No idea how it happened; I just woke with it' –
As you stand at a distance for a moment, observing me
As if outside glass. I ask you to come with me
And we drive out and back the way we walked,
Only fast now – the other way in reverse –
Covering over yesterday as I put my foot down
And the land speeds flat through our eyes, rewinding
Towards two waiting figures we stop to let in –
On their way back from the Island, to Raasay,
To the Manse there. You chat to them,
And the name lingers in the Orkney mists
In the salt breath of rasping, singing silence.

We come into Bunessan, and it's over in minutes,
By a white house round the bay from the heron:

The portacabin surgery door, the torch-piece probe,
The clear glutinous drops, and a plug of cotton wool;
Two days, she pronounces ... the remaining time.

We head back, meet you coming the other way,
Mira. You stretch up your smiling thumb
On the way we're going, to the Island of Dreams,
To the dream that will reach your deep brown eyes;
We take you the last mile to the jetty,
Turning back like a taxi paid in warmth, not money.

I name this a Doing Nothing day,
A Sabbath where there is none, only the sun
And the blue of the sky drawing us seawards
To the Island like a ramp of floating blue air –
An invisible jetty in the mind's eye of cloud

       wisps of woven floated cirrus, suspended

Upended above the road's end we have seen.
As I write to you now, all the air spells it:

'I have seen the mountain: now is the climb'

Where there's no handhold or foothold but breath
And what was fasting and praying – attuning now
Into the inner being of the sky.

What was your command, Lord? How did you know
To make this water into wine, and the waters stir,
And the loaves and fishes multiply? I AM –
Ego eimi – and the words untranslatable,
As they are in the mouth of the blind beggar seeing
Who knows what they mean and who can say no other
And whose eyes are full of light and the day
They are blind to as they gaze at him, and You in him –

'I am the Way, the Truth, and the Life'

— and the Dream of Life: and we are,
And You are the blue and the gold in all of us
Becoming us like the sky's breath.

Do nothing: only resurrect
Do nothing: only see the day as it is
And you will know the meaning of dreaming.

I close the book, and find you —
And we decide to wander on down to Fionnphort
To walk the last of the road we began: the sky opens
On the breath of the breeze it carries towards us,
Softening our eyes, weighed by our luggage
So that it weighs and yet doesn't weigh in our hands.
We pass outside the café and we find you, Margot,
Sitting at a table with the sun on your face;
You turn and gesture us to join you, waving.

We sit with coffee, and you talk about Tagore
And Mozart, the child of light, and his daimon —
And Tennyson, in his melancholy … a silence comes
As imperceptibly as hearing that we are talking *words*
Not feelings, not this moment, not listening — not *this* —
And it steals over me: I have to stand and walk away
A few yards, as if someone is trying to talk to me,
Something in the light is saying, *'Listen — '*
All over my left side, like a slanting brightness:

Ring your mother

So how do I do that?! She's in the light —
Shining down on to my body … and yet I seem to know
As I see a phone dial, old style, like a joke: three letters on it.
I raise my finger to it, daft and simple as it is,

And dial it, G.O.D. – and it's you
As immediately as I can breathe, before I can even think,
Saying you will be with me there –

You there, as suddenly as you were in light
And as suddenly as you come now ... the line dissolves,
The telephone, your voice, everything, into this
After-echo of your precise inaudible being
Filling the light around my head, and filling me –

The lines of cars like abandoned egos glittering in the sun,
Parked before the jetty where the ferry has gone ...
I come back to you and smile and nod
                              saying nothing;

We walk out to find a place to sit
Away from the noise – leaving you to return.
We cross the narrow strip of beach with its blond sand
And climb up over the grass, among the rocks,
Until we find one facing the right way, to the Island
Rising sheer behind us like a vertical cliff face
Up into the sky with its cirrus, above its edge.
We lean our backs into it ...
                              as I read

And you drift with your kerchief
Tied around your head in the sun ...

                              and you sleep, then

Your breathing deepens and changes.
I glance at the side of your face –

And I find the word and the wood I am looking for
Without even knowing it

          when the page opens and sings 'Raasay'

In your clear ringing voice, Sorley Maclean,
In your pure octave of full-felt feeling
As vertical as the rock behind me,
And line by line you nod beside me …

> '*I took my way*
> *through the restless intricacy;*
> *I took the course*
> *through the new land of dream*'

As the whole of the wood breathes in the inner air
Inside the sun

      glittering on the Sound …

And in the wind's breath and the touch of grass
By my hand,
As the whole of my voice rises in yours
Sung as if in tongues
                from a mountain stream

> '*You were eloquent at evening*
> *with songs in your house*
> *and cool with dews*
> *silently falling* …'

And the sun begins to drift in me, under my eyelids,
As your breathing steadies

      and your head leans sideways

And the words begin to blur into green,
Into the green of the light that is the grass-lit sun

> '*The woods of Raasay,*
> *my dear prattler,*

my whispered reason,
my sleeping child ...'

While the page lies lined, and open, and empty
And the air ruffles under it

                  as I close my eyes ...

Green-shot light ...

                the silent waves ...

                          and the breath

            from across the water:

From somewhere in the dream a voice begins to speak,
Not in words, but in a pure metre of feeling –
From the poem as it is, dreamt beyond thinking
As its seeing and sensing, all at once, flood over me:

I am drawn into a dream
where I see you standing
in the circle of the mountain:
rocks and grasses, and you
invisibly in green, my face.

Then you dissolve, and only
your voice remains —
rapid in image after image
you speak through ...

'Let everything go
that separates you from this.'

Words I cannot remember or name,
sounds and scents and gestures
woven in light, like a woman's hair

as I move down threads of grasses
as she works her fingers through me

and I vanish to myself — I become the dream
that the breeze and the glittering sea
slowly draw me back from
as you say

'*Void and fill-bearer,*
let the Summerland whisper to you.'

Your head touches and rests on my shoulder

And void and fill-bearer is all I am

                             as we come to and

You stretch to move —
'What have you been doing?'
I tell you the dream, and you tell me yours of expanding
Where you left your body through your eyes —
Becoming everything you were seeing:

The Dream
                the Dream of Life

— dissolving us beyond ourselves

And loosening us
                as all the levels blend ...

Seeing it like lightning as we stand,
Dry summer lightning, half-hidden behind your eyes,
Flickering and vanishing into itself
                            blond light, blond sand ...

We decide to walk to Red Bay overland
In our own time. You reflect, 'It can't be far –'
Facing the rocks and grasses where there's no path,
Only the outline of outcrops and free stretches of grass.
We enter this pathless land where, we could have guessed,
It soon becomes impossible to walk in a straight line;
We zig-zag inland from the cliffs, hugging the edge
And skirting the rocks where the ground soaks to bog
To wade in down through the waist-high bracken …

And with every rise we come to it's further;
There's only the pink cracked craggy stone, like flesh,
More untrodden bracken and bog, more of the same,
And then it's like a dream where we're getting nowhere
However far we go, the landscape isn't changing,
And it seems we've gone no distance from where we started;
There's no way of saying how far it is now.
We closen to a house roof we think must be it,
But it isn't! So then we have to let go

To this unknown will guiding us
To walk without faith, hope or fear
                    and Be Lost

As the whole landscape becomes like a heart
Like yours or mine, with its peaks and troughs.
Where we come down to the Bay of No Name
We find an unspoilt beach where nobody goes, only sheep,
Which I call the Bay of Treasures, where you find shells
You could have covered your nipples with
And seaweed you could be laced with, like an undine,
Over your soft white unresisting body
As I see you walking in yourself, alone.

When we climb back up, the sheep show us the way,
Starting, startled, out of the adder-grass

162

Where they've been lying, hidden as we are
In the jungle of our moistness and our dreaming
Where their round bobs of shit gleam in the sun.

The ground opens and flattens, and we see the house
Beyond two pylons and a broken line of wall
I cross like a dotted line, between its stones ...
And I glance down, and you do too:
We find them, one by one, littered here and there,
Some broken, some whole, bent, or intact
And some in a cluster fallen together –
Eagle's feathers! We hold them, wondering.
You smooth down one its length to its tip

> *And the eagle had hovered*
> *over us in the sun*

> *And the broken eagle*
> *had risen, and flown*

His wings stretching out with the sun on him,
And we stand on the spot where his clawed feet landed.

Coming through, we join you
Sitting outside on the grass in the sun as you wave
In the light, in the goldening light, over the bay
Where the Island and the rocks blaze in a lens of glass:
'So you came in by the back door! How was it?'
'Thorough,' I quip, leaving you to talk about it

As I lean against the wall to take some space
To draft these lines: I glimpse your face in profile
As you sit in front of me, Rosemary, listening ...
With the sun in your hair, softening your eyes
Until I'm seeing you in your beauty, as I want you to –
I reach for the camera as you blink and turn

And it's gone in a moment, gone for ever,
Telling me again *how feeling comes first*
And last, faster than any finger can freeze it.

I put the pen down, and a large tawny orange tom
Comes over nuzzling against my knee
And sprawls out flatly like a lion on the page,
Refusing to budge, so I can't write another word,
Hand moving to ruffle his kingly fur ...

You turn to me, Christine, and tell me
About your friend who had a baby who died in six months
And all she could say, even through her grief,
Was *Thank God we had him so long*. As you add,
'I've never got over that,' your eyes glisten

Gratitude – how else can it be,
Seeing the warm sun over your backs
As you share a poem you're writing together,
Josephine, with your hair loose and open
A white yard long, almost touching the grass?
Gratitude, thanks, and praise be this moment
And for freeing my hands to feel it as it lingers,
Knowing it, even as we sit in it
In this sunlight weaving its warm spell
So we don't even have to name it
                                    gratitude, praise

The two keys transformed
And the door open flooding with light –
The door that is no door, but islands, miles wide,
While the bay sparkles
                        and the truth is crystalline

And the light on the water
                        glows incandescent

As you stand by the wall, all of you – for this.
I count your faces smiling, laughing and ducking,
Or just looking quietly ahead,
And you, Ann, like a heart at the centre
Among the living and the dying and the dead
Seeing us as we see you, *in the light*, then,
As no one else can see us, like ageless children
Who have never grown out of the end of ourselves,
Only to die and grow younger and deepen
Until we're no age at all, only what we're feeling,
Only and ever – this is our communion
Before we eat and feast on the fading light
Before the earth darkens for its last longest season.

We will have seen this, so we can remember it: union,
The glimmer of the hope of it that is untrying
That pours like the light out of a jug of air
Over the lip of itself, a free careless blessing.

We sit inside as you tell me, David,
About flying a thousand feet over the desert
Like a sea of wavelets, where a sandstorm had been,
Where it looked as though a long bag had been dragged …
You talk about Africa, written in your face
Like the best you've had, that's never left you,
And when I ask you how you see your patients you remark,
'Everyone wears a mask, but they drop it when they come in'
And the light glances off the edge of your smile
As if it could be as simple as faith –

And the light is smiling, even in you, Tom,
When you talk about us all and tell us your truth
And we open our eyes – and I see the heaviness
Around your shoulders that it breaks through; we thank you
And three lines come like a claidon I give you
And now I tell myself –

Put the burden down
And it becomes the mountain
You climb up to your freedom

                         — as I see you there.

After all the names we can name, there's you
Where no one at that height has a name, or needs one
Under the open eye we come to stretched like the sky.
Even Schumacher, as you tell us, Duncan,
Was harvested drunk after his finest speech;
So who can say what greatness is
But to give the whole of yourself into the end,
To give the whole of your heart, and go.
Is that all we shy from? And all we can know ...

The light gone rose over the bay
In fold after fold distended across the horizon like an answer
And the rocks gone quiet to it, the rocks in shadow —
The sky flung wide seeping wine through every crevice.

Day 17

Fionnphort – Iona

Rushing light
                racing ... to pack up and leave.

    We go down to try and find where you left your camera
Somewhere among the rocks, in daylight now,
The light shimmering as we drive under a clear cloudless sky
Of vivid deep cerulean blue
                        clear for the crossing ...

We come to the beach before the climb
Where the jellyfish lie stranded on the dry tide-sand
Like discs of clear spittle
                        pink-starred
                    at their centres

And we pause ...

Before the tract of rock and grass opens
Among scattering sheep ... and you go on ahead.
Miraculously, improbable as it seems,
You're guided to the very spot where you left it
(Unhesitatingly, as if you already knew).
You had no idea how, and you never will,
Only that your mind was empty and you let go ...

We drive back fast on the road round to the bay
To pick the others up. The cows come ambling, Jersey-brown,
To stand and gaze, blocking the road, unmoving;
Giving me stillness as I breathe and let go, too.

Two signs for the crossing:
We stand around, and the little ferry comes in
No bigger than a coracle, it seems.
We queue vaguely to the left, out of the way
With space for one car and its trailer, if you're lucky.
I'm watching an old bearded sea dog, with his large bare arms,
Thin wind-blown hair, standing, chatting;
He could be Columba's brother in disguise ...
These things precious as the car backs off,
The loose things are handed out in boxes,
And the postman's new bike, in cardboard, goes on,
Then we step on to the floating deck, one by one
Into the narrowing eyes, like a needle ...
Carrying what's light
                              with the rest inside us.

The craft draws out and turns, immediately reversing
One eighty, like a slow spinning
Under the turning sky above, where the rest is done
As you face forward for this brief passage
With your head still raised, like a drunkard
Full of wind, and sea, and sky, and I breathe
And the breath of the Sound opens out through my lungs:

Lord, be in my breathing
Lord, be in my being
Lord, be in my speech
                              as the song drifts from within

Strong in my body from head to feet,
Hovering, to its wings

With what can't pass through the eye, like the Sound,
And what can
                    and can only
                              and that is freedom

The freedom that can breathe, and be, holding nothing
— *so it is all gift, all given* —

Then I am the one You made me
By this breath, under this sky. As it fills me
We stand and face the brightening shore like a dream:

White sand, the handful of houses against the rock ...
— the oldest rock in the world, risen above the sea —
And we come to land at the brief concrete jetty
The green ramp's lowered on ...
                                                            I walk

Feeling my first steps touching the ground,
Yours beside me silently, under your bursting voices,
I put my bag and rucksack down, and in a second
I turn and spin round, reaching out my arms
Without a second thought as the ground takes me ...

Our steps slow in the dream as we file
Towards habitation: the very ground is different;
It's as if you can feel your whole body fluidly
Inside your legs and feet in the blue of the sun,
And the far shore is a dream, the luggage is a dream,
As we straggle apart, in a loose line —
Past the Argyll Hotel and the sign for the Abbey
Where a woman stands in her garden, the sea glitters,
And the ground opens into a rough grass field
By the side of the boundary wall that leads
Where I watch your drifting figures wandering ahead
As part of the breath of the air that fills you
As we take our last steps into this beginning:

The Abbey walls rising as we round the gate,
Its patched pink and grey cemented stone under the blue
To its box-tower clock with its runic woven knot

Where time is, and stands still: vertical, white –
The whole tower like a dovecote for white, white wings
As they settle invisibly along the roof lines
Flaking in the light, part of its glare.
We glance at St Martin's Cross on its pedestal –
Weathered, slate-grey, for eleven centuries
Evaporating into the blue of the day and *now, now*
With its encircled dots and bosses, gleaming
Where the sky and each moment is stronger than stone.

We circle round it, weaving to the cloister door
And down the steps into its cool green courtyard
Flanked by shadow – and in the centre of the grass the sun –
Where *The Descent of the Spirit* stands, in green bronze,
Lit from behind, like a drooping egg
                                        to this birthing

And we wait, welcomed –
Then into the Chapter House to gather
On chairs in front of its clear glass windows …

We sit silently, breathing in the dream
That is the faintest sound of the sea where the quietness hangs,
Breathing to its slow curl and fall, with the sun, sun
Outside streaming in at our backs on to the carpet.
We surface one by one to speak or stay silent:
You point to the woven strands in their rich pattern,
Asking that we may be *as aware* as them
In the joy and sadness of living, where they're one,
Each needing the other, as we do,
And I watch the dream in front of your eyes that we are:

'*O God help me to be in the present moment*
To let go of what has gone
And not to worry about what is to come …'

As the lines well in front of you, for all of us,
We breathe with relief and smile at your almost-tears,
Your face reddening as if in embarrassment,
And the pull at my navel strengthens like an ache
To give birth to what I can't yet see

for the Kingdom

That begins with each one of us
In the depth of our innermost need.

And outside we wander, now with time
Because there's nowhere else to go now, but Now
Still the sea, glittering

and the far shore like a dream

The breeze, everywhere

its warmth quietening us, 'only listen'

And where she stands, with her hands poised,
Palms open –
The dove descending above her head,
The hollow channel reaching down through her thighs,
And round, like an inverted heart, that is her sitting,
Squatting, with the mystery of her thighs open
And the creatures groaning and kneeling beneath her
As the pure world streams down through her
From the dove's upended beak –
As she sits, Everywoman, like a virgin queen

And I gaze, as I will repeatedly, again

At her

kneeling to Him

And Him

kneeling to wash your feet ...

I wander through the cloister again
Towards the bookshop, under its narrow cornice arch,
Where I find you, Sheila, behind the counter.
You smile welcome and our eyes meet
And what it is I recognise about you because I don't?
What is it about your boyish brown hair
And shining eyes, standing in the brightness of yourself,
That makes you seem to have come from another world?
'I always know a Londoner when I meet one,' I joke,
And is it because there's nothing of the past about you
In the clearness of your voice and seeing eyes?
Somewhere, you have broken as free as the day,
Uniquely yourself, boy-woman, androgyne.

Already as I leave I want to come back again
And you follow me out invisibly to the sun
The way a dream does, the way I lose and find you,
In that perfect time where we're all held ...

Three women travellers asleep in the light,
Rucksacks beside them, under Columba's mount,
Stretched out on the trust of the ground ...
I walk to the Coffee House to find you, Val,
By the window with a cooling cup
And you show me the page you're reading:

Mount Carmel

With the map John drew, *'for my daughter, Magdalen'*
Written at its foot, its ascending lines like pillars
Entering the infinite circle through the centre,
Through the Nothing of the Night of his narrow path
— *'nothing, nothing, even on the mount, nothing'* —
To where *'The honour and glory of God alone dwell ...'*
And I think of the mountain

there is to climb now

Up inside each other's heart
And not out of this world, but *into* it

                              for humanity

As I lean against a balustrade of the Abbey,
Watching the sun ruffling the brightening grass ...

I slip round the side to the Michael Chapel
And in through its studded door, lifting its iron hasp,
To stand for a moment among the empty pews
Where the stillness hangs at the edge, waiting
As the light brightens over the sea beyond the glass ...

You shiver down in me in the shape of the window
You gentle shimmering sword of down-showering light

Mich-ael, in the silence

                    real as your name

And as the One you serve:
'This is your attuning'

And all I want to do is sleep! Or dream,
Staying with the inner feeling of the dream,
Not asleep but awake ... and not speaking but speechlessly

Be in the Beginning of Everything
Because under this sky it can all be spoken
Under this blue it can all be shown

We file into the refectory to eat

                    among its long tables and announcements

And now I walk to phone you, tell you we've arrived
 – rounding the bright boundary wall of the Nunnery –
The money vanishing out of my fingers to the pips ...

You say the one word you will always say,
'Mother', to remind me — of the heart-thread,
Your voice softening me, always to this centre
Which is the only true story I've ever lived.

I walk back, to the grass, to sleep,
To stretch out to the sea-sound
With the blue stretched like an eye above my head;
An eye and an ear.
                           It's where the blue touches you,
It's where the sea, the silver sea, says, 'Listen'

And it's where I let go to my body
                                      to this Body
I blend into till I become its edges,
That it begins:

Blue windows, like stained glass, in the darkness
Blue-filled with the light of their shape
Split either side of a line of darkness
                                      as they hover

And it's time to begin the mountain.

Dun I: crouched behind the Abbey from the sea,
Once a hill fort, before any of these buildings rose,
It masses like the base of an invisible peak,
Which its pinnacle marker pins the centre of,
Reaching beyond into the air, like the eagle's wings
Spread out where the blue haze blends sea, horizon, island:

And it waits, like the breeze, saying nothing but *begin me.*
Begin the climb up through yourself, beyond you.

I walk up the one fenced road that's a lane
Passing the mound of the Vallum,

174

Out of earshot to the breeze, each dense step
Falling into a different rhythm that is the air's.
I branch left over a stile to the field's edge
That leads past the sheep to where the hill rises
Shouldering high over a tiny gouged stream
And an outcrop of broken rocks I touch with my hands.

Hands and feet, to climb with – to touch the hill's
Grass-green warmth tussock by tussock, to lever up
Among its loose scree of stones where I am *on its body*, yours.
Your breath breathes me in the breaths I take;
You soak in through every pore of my skin and eyes,
Green mountain: green rising into the blue, the whole journey
Come to your base, gathered in your body now
Gleaming with yellow buttercups, like the light of it,
And mauve-sheathed harebells, crocus-fragile,
White stars swallowed in the tiniest of flowers
Whiter than stone with light, greeting my face.

I will go half way, and no further. Not yet.
I come to a ledge of grass the width of a bed,
Sheltered by rock, under its overhang ... to pause,
To rest and let go more deeply again
To the grass that says *lie on me* as the flowers say *wild*

And the Island stretches out below
                    over the red roofs of the farm buildings

The rough map of the sunlit fields
                    over Lochan Mor, dry now

Beyond to the blue of the Sound ...
                    Aegean turquoise

Over to Mull and the Abbey roof
                    beyond to the hills of Jura

Haunting the skyline, translucent.

I lie down and let it go ... and you, there ... everything I know
To this, for this – where all I ask You is
Let me be here as You want me to be, to receive.

Where I come to the end of my being
                    and at the end of my dreams
                                        You come

You come as you came and will always come
In the heart of our surrender that is love
In the inner thread of its being that is freed,
Taking us beyond the edge of the sky, even
Further than anything can see – and further here
Than a grassblade trembling, or a leaf

          where the eye crosses that same distance:

You who are more earthly and heavenly than we dare to be
Come, Creator, come
Come, Lord of Love, come

Descending, the distant bell
Waking me at six, the grass still warm on me,
I come down with the edge of the sky around me
                                        to find you

For the third time today, and we arrange to meet.
You don't seem surprised, as if expecting me,
Although it's not in what you say and wasn't in your mind
As you whiled away the time till closing time,
But in the energy between our eyes that says *there is a path*
And all we have to do is walk it, and see.

I come back to the hubbub of voices
I lose your face and form in –
Where it's all of us, in the floating community
Standing, queuing, bowed over clattering cutlery
Filling the ark of the roof that's landed here ...
On the benches, our faces lifted under the blue,
Full of the brightness of the day like a grace.
And as we talk, Mae, you say, 'The voice is bigger than we know,
Invisible as it is; it's our whole being resonating'
As we journey to the I am that echoes from our names.

We're going into the Evening Service,
Filing in through the side door of the cloister
Which opens on to the flagstones at the crossing's edge
Where the Abbey's lit depth reaches down to the altar
And its silver cross gleaming in the silver window-light
Under the tended clean stone arches, and the
Candles above the pews picking out their varnish,
As the piano begins high up in the loft –
And on the pulpit a deep gold cross bright as a key
With the sunlight slanting gold through the windows behind.

We give each other a sign of welcome,
Turning to our neighbour as our friend – it's easy,
You wouldn't think twice before doing it – *it's You*
In all the ordinary moments we can remember to say so
And now I know I'm home as I've never been
In any church or temple, as we face forward together,
Home where it's natural to be, with nothing forced
As the whole Island speaks in through the walls

And in your voice as you say

'I look to the mountains –
where will my help come from?
My help will come from the Lord

who made heaven and earth ...'

Raising your head back, your fine red hair resting
Down on your shoulders, your full woman's throat bared

As we sing a Song of Blessing, our voices reaching
High up into the golden and silver warmth
The candlelight flickers in, under the shadow of the stone
That's been built, and levelled, and rebuilt from a shell
So it holds us now without pretence or grandeur –
And even as we speak the Lord's Prayer it stays,
Relaxed in our voices, as you speak in our voices,
As you would say it to a friend – Friend as He is
And Stranger, as you tell us, and we say

WE SAW A STRANGER YESTERDAY
WE PUT FOOD IN THE EATING PLACE
DRINK IN THE DRINKING PLACE
MUSIC IN THE LISTENING PLACE

And you remind us, sister

As the lark sings in her song
Often, often, often goes the Christ in the stranger's guise

And we sing now

The Spirit lives to set us free
Walk, walk in the light
And binds us all in unity
Walk, walk in the light

WALK IN THE LIGHT
WALK IN THE LIGHT
WALK IN THE LIGHT OF THE LORD

While it's still light –
'I am with you but a little while ...'

I come outside to find you in the cloister
Under the yellow shadow of its eaves.
'I heard you singing,' you say as we pause for a moment
On the bench, looking down at our feet,
Then we head back through the walkway and out
Past the broken shaft of St Matthew's Cross
With its fragment of Adam and Eve, where we linger ...

'Shall we walk north?' 'You be my guide.'
We step into the wind, in the gathering twilight,
Up the lane that leads to the mountain, and past it
As you talk about the need for space for communing ...
Then we glance across at the sky,
The first hint of amber gold on the horizon
Over the fence and darkening field, and we slow
To the crack of light the sky has opened: we stand
And I feel your standing by me silently as we gaze

And why, but there are tears in the beauty,
I feel them pricking ... and you seem to know.
The skein of the light touches the skin of my eyes,
Touches my face as they well, and want to, and not in pain now
And you almost reach to touch my arm, and stop.
It was the temple of the sky going on for ever.
I say, 'I know it,' and I can't say more

The thin path stretching as we stretch our legs
With others there, crossing the field ahead ...
Their shadows move into the beauty, and vanish
To the outline of the air and the ground. We follow them
And the sky closens and there's no need to talk,
Only to feel each other's silence, and this

As we cross into the field and you unhook the gate,
The gate you are: to where the land opens on to the sea,
The sea, the sea at last coming to meet us.
You say, 'I've never seen it as clear as this – '
And we barely know the grass beneath our feet as we cross it.

We slip through a gap round the side of a small tied gate
And then round a dark mound
Towards the bay, the sand, and the rocks, and you say,
'It's extraordinary, not even the rocks are quite real.
Look, they're almost silver!' and they are
 – framed against the light, and within it –
And the sea a molten blue
                        folding in …

And the sky scored in shards of rose, like delicate blades

Where the islands are floating
                        Staffa, Lunga, Reidh

Then the colour I glance up into is *green*,
A lingering rising green sheen as the tears come again
And the light lingering gold, so I know
                        this is real

And the gulls glide silently overhead
Shadowed against the deep, deep blue of the upper air
As you go into the picture, on to the sand – you stand
So lightly silhouetted and so light.
You are a present and a future being, facing out

And your threshold is bird's feet webbed in the sand I cross,
The sand alive with sand-midges, jumping,
As I stand apart from you; we each stand alone

And how can I say it, being wordless and dumb
With wings that want to stretch open in my heart,
But *'thank you'* with my eyes to you –
Can only turn as I do, without touching you,
Can only turn wanting to cry into the sun-rose light
To say *my heart's being broken through my eyes*
As if broken again; but, no, healed to stretch and sing
An unknown song welling in my throat

      the song You are breaking me to sing.

How can I say it? But with this pebble
I turn up that is Iona greenstone
I trace an encircled cross … letting the sand be this page,
And you bend and turn up one that's jet black
To draw a circle with, and two lines within,
Like a dancing curve, a dancing foot's pirouette …
Now there's something at the apex but I can't see it.
It's radiant – look – and I don't know its shape
But it's a kind of star raying down on both of us
As we stand back looking at what we've made.

Then enough: it's done, you smile, we turn to go,
But as we leave the shore and glance back on the grass
The sky won't leave us, it's not letting us go,
Deepening into full-blown rose …
Behind it, a stretch of mottled cloud like an island,
An island of rose, of its own
                like Hy-Brasil –

Then rising deep out of its glow – first one band
Then another – and another – like the ends of rainbows
Projected up, arcing from under the horizon –
Streaking the thin unbelievable air in blue and then pink
In rays you have to look twice to see

As they dissolve

        then appear again

And to the far west in the smoky grey
The sun has gone, leaving a raying star of colour
Spreading at its edges like tentacles of light
And it *is* a star

        but we don't know its form, remember.

We turn now: its pure gift asking for nothing.
What else is there to say? And we walk

But my tongue is numb with beauty
My tongue has been struck dumb with beauty

'You've opened my heart – and the sky.'
You walk quietly, knowing, and neither of us knowing
Or even knowing each other – like you, Stranger –
And you look down and shy your glance away
And all we can do is trust what comes between us
Given, as it is

        on the first day we were made.

In the dark ... as we skirt past the Nunnery,
Where a single red light is glowing like a star –
And in the dark I walk back to the monastery;
Silhouetted figures on the hill's edge, by the gateway ruin,
Like ours – *and you know, we were never alone.*

Day 18

Iona

Silver dawn, waking
                    behind my eyes

A silver sea flowing in through the light

        like light from beyond the sky

        inaudibly whispering … as I fall asleep again

Filling the windows, brightening now
From their first mist-likeness, glimmering with the water.

Sunday 9 a.m. when the bell goes for breakfast
I go in reluctantly … the chores looming!
Behind the old raised dais platform in the kitchen
I'm slicing a vat of potatoes and watching the blade
As the segments crowd into lines: and you chop, chop away
Beside me, chatting – you and Canon O., the uptight priest
Who regards all semblance of ecstasy with suspicion
Behind his round, polished, orderly, too-clean glasses …
Ah, and it is fear makes Pharisees of us all
And if it isn't my idea of how you spend a morning
'It ain't what you want, it's what you need' – perfection.

I wonder about you as I wonder about him – polarity –
And how You come through all of us – and if You don't
Surely it's because we aren't our actual selves?
You had no artifice about you on any Sunday.
Look how we get stuck in roles – poet and priest –
While there's a humanness reaching under both like a knife
That needs all our differences to open, and to see

Why we meet each other when we do, with news.
(Have I got news for you!)

Humanness-communion and Wholly Communion,
The Dream of Unity that grists us to its mill –
And all we have to do is learn to love, and let go
And keep loving and letting go all the way down the line.
What stops me loving is all I need to know
Again and again, and again now. Truth.

We go into Communion in the daylight Abbey
With its slate stone and red granite, like a heart
Opening up to enfold us under its vault – in the flame,
The soft flame of hands in prayer, in the arch ...
You begin, Ali, where you left off
While the light gleams through the windows behind you:

Thanks be to you O God that we have risen this day

And we add

TO THE RISING OF THIS LIFE ITSELF

                        yay!

    Be the purpose of God between us, and each purpose

THE HAND OF GOD BETWEEN US AND EACH HAND

                            as I see yours

    The pain of Christ between us and each pain

THE LOVE OF CHRIST BETWEEN US AND EACH LOVE

                            as You fill me

    Beloved of the waifs, beloved of the naked

                  as You touch me

DRAW US TO THE SHELTER HOUSE OF THE SAVIOUR OF THE
    POOR

– that is us, in soul and spirit as we sing
And our voices rise, trembling and clear, like the waves
As the daylight lifts in each of us, in our mouths,
And what surrender it is to sing,
To be that vulnerable and unafraid
As our hearts open to the Song like a whale
In the Body we are, down the length of the nave into the choir –

And you say

    God, holy

        and we say

GOD STRONG AND HOLY
GOD, HOLY AND DEATHLESS
HAVE MERCY ON US

And you add, in the pause, as the air hovers over us

    Listen now, for God speaks to us in the scriptures

As I listen to Corinthians and Mark
I think of the Gospel of the Living Breath
Moment by moment, scored on the living air ...
And as the words blur and blend in their litany
All I hear is all I need to hear, while the rest falls away:

    'Whoever does what God wants him to do is my
    brother, my sister, my mother ...'

– and then we are Your Family
        as strangely we find our way alone

and in finding You find each other
as naked as your face is, now ...

Where else do we find You but *here*, however here is,
As we sing it:

The God of Heaven is present on earth
In word and silence and sharing,
In face of doubt, in depth of faith
In signs of love and caring ...

And you stand to speak, now —
You stand, a woman in the pulpit, in your ordinary clothes
With your face as grave and alive and awake, only more so,
So much more so
                    as the delight of you ripples back to me

And to *you*, beside me as you nod and smile.

You talk about difference and denial,
Or our idolisation of it, which is just the same —
And how what we miss in each is the living truth
That we are *each* unique, each different and beloved
And as unique and as different as we are. Seeing it,
We were each called into relationship with You —
The You that you call *'the living God'*, which echoes,
Yes, the God that is alive beyond all our thinking ...

And community? You fill out the theme
'The New Covenant is also with community —'
Which means we need each other, so we are here together,
And not just for each other, but for ourselves in You,
The Body that is You, mirroring us to ourselves,
And the Body we can only love beyond ourselves —
So, as you say, *it's neither collective nor individual;*

Community rests in the tension in between
And needs the tension in between, like a drawn bow —

Alone, and in company, and alone together
Like lovers for the work — as I love your voice,
Its fine, dignified phrasing — its warmth, its passion,
And its lightness that only a royal woman has.
You have it, and you have us in the palm of your hand
As you raise it to gesture the shape of the cross,
Upwards and across, where the breathing centre is,
That is rose and liquid fire and strangeness,
Poetry and prose and the living Word, alive in you.

And where are we living? In the tension
That is bearing the burden of the New Life, bearing it,
And we cannot live there without justice
And we cannot live there without mercy ... your words burn,
And we cannot live there without the Spirit, which means
We're in communion with each other, and we need help:

Holy Spirit, binding all reality together,
Which all our connections and threads are sacred to,
Be with us, breathe down through us, I want to say,
'Because from here comes the urge to heal what is broken.'

Ah, and in your lightness now

   'Seek justice, live generously, and seek out the Spirit'

You step down, and we pray,
Listing the names and places when you pause,
And the darkness behind our eyes is a still deep warmth
While we bow our heads, kneeling or sitting, and you say

'We are embodied with them now ...'

– and a green key of light glimmers in two tiny windows –

And *lachma*, the body needs bread;
It needs the Bread that is coming now –

'Look, here is Christ coming …'

You pass it back in torn brown hunks
Tanned deep as a desert and like bread from a feast,
Fresh, soft, and yeasty as You are rich,
Giving everything and holding nothing back –
And the golden chalice cup goes from hand to hand in silence

And oh, your bread was brown grain
And your wine was liquid honey

                              my Lord, she sang

And we speak THE BLESSING OF THE GOD OF LIFE

– the grains still under my teeth and tongue.

We stand and leave the building in the sun.
As I pass the pulpit I see your text has come true,
Isaiah, old fiery one –

My word shall not return unto me void

– gouged in the living wood, the tree's tattoo.

As we sit in the refectory,
Amidst the stirring swell of our voices,
I glance up at the shelf in front of the high window
Where a cross has been carved out of a slab of rock –
Laid in relief against it, rising as if out of it.
When your voice goes silent beside me I see
That the Cross has shattered in the Rock

188

And as it breaks, You are raised, You are lifted up,
You are lifted out of time, lifted free,
And Your Stone, this Island stone, is the Rock of Ages
And Your Rock, this ancient rock, is the Rock of Ages:

You are the sky now where the eagle drifts,
The Song drifts
                    and the Song is —

    and the dove flies with its message in its beak

    — in timeless time, in white sky between sky —

Where Your Outline shoulders all of this ...

I go outside to take some space,
Rounding the cloister and out on the gravel path.
Seven white doves fringe the grass edge, picking,
Where the blue Island bus is parked beside the wall;
They nose and wander, fan-tails spread ...

I round the Abbey and stand
Inside the Chapel for a moment:
A waterfall plunges
                    in front of the windows

In a single stream of blue light through the darkness —

And it's time to go back to the mountain.

The lane quiet in the afternoon light,
Treading the pathway, knowing it now,
Calling the mountain my Hall of Learning
As you might have done, Columba. I take you with me
To read, sleep, or dream — whatever the mountain brings —
Passing you in silence. Walking towards me,

Like brother to brother you nod, not wanting to speak.
I watch your colours drifting forward into the haze
Towards the north shore or the White Strand, as it takes you,
As I branch left again to climb up halfway.

The sheep nibbling in the heat, the water trickling,
Grass warm to the touch – and the clover, this time
As I wind up zigzagging between the outcrops,
Pausing to feel you breathing into my heart
Like these yellow flowers I can't name that gleam like fire.

I'm sitting leaning back against the overhang
While the day hangs below down the grassy slope
Over the stone lip of a hill on its own –
To where the side of a house is lit up like a white triangle:
And beyond it over the water at the edge of the bay
The terraces of the Bourg rise to Ben More
Under a stretch of low broad cloud swathing its peak.

I read about you again, after a gap of twelve years,
Wondering at how the man of war became a Prince of Peace,
How all that anger in you was transformed,
How Eithne knew to call you *Dove*,
How Finnian saw a sky with two moons, one like a sun …
I can almost see your large grey luminous eyes
That knew you from the beginning, and which you became,
Bowed after Culdreihmne, so you set sail to here,
Island by island till Ireland was out of sight –

The Sea of God taking your fragile coracle.
I glance down – these are your flowers!
Yours and the Baptist's. You carried them in your habit,
Your rough woollen habit, in the rain like a ghost and
Lying on your bed you made out of broad flat stone …

And as the sun blazes I can almost hear
Your clear ringing voice across the Sound to Mull
'Reprimanding some unfortunate', like a Zen master
Alive in the air and the ground, bridging heaven,
Driving around in your little cart, old father ...

And when I glance up, into your face
Comes a single white horse clopping down the lane
With no rider and no guide, his hooves following,
His back and mane gleaming in the sun

                             knowing the way

As I descend towards him

And now I must ascend again.

A black cross lowered into very deep water, blue water
And a naked crucified figure turning
And struggling to break free, come exhaustedly down

Up now past the overhang
To where the last stretch leads up to the cairn
As the wind rises over the grass, the rough ground levels,
To the look-out point like an I, as sky and sea open:
I tread the last steps, breathing, buoyant in air,
To the roof of the world and the centre

                         where the four directions

Span out like a huge cross the Island encircles,
Circling them at its centre
As the eagle invisibly circles

                         and the flowers gleam:

I stand in the silence, the wind and the sun.
This is the place, the least and the last
Where the greatest is and I am empty, I am nothing;

see through me

North
        where the ground dips towards the white shore

   to Staffa, Rhum, and the Sgurr of Eigg

And the dim blue of the Cuillins on Skye where the sky blends

South
        where the sea silvers to a liquid glare

    over the foreground etched in rainbow and the Torran Rocks

To Colonsay and Jura in a blaze of white cloud

East
        to the Ross of Mull, over the red rocks …

   where the sea is as calm as a mirror to the breath

And the mountains' height is combed free, like a veil, and

West
        where the seals beach and the blowhole spouts

   into the open sea that is unbroken

Until it reaches two thousand miles to America

— as I turn
        and turn again
                and turn again round

Arms outstretched as if through my eyes
— to the northwest shore where we stood last night —

192

Towards a higher earth
                    where the islands are not islands

Or land as we have thought it to be …

And beyond the islands
                    in the haze where sky meets sea

There is land, and it is not Ireland.

                    You said, it is the Kingdom
                    and there is no end to the Kingdom

And the phrase you whisper is *'Dreams out of Time'*
On this Island of Dreams
                    and it is the Summerland

And the Summerland we're in.

Sitting by the cairn, I see
That it can't be coerced into song,
It has to be let go to, and wholly:
I must be open to receive
Whatever You choose to show me
And let it surprise me, let it
Stun me, let it quieten me …

And I should be able to come all this way
Just to find a single yellow flower
And for that to be enough

St John's Wort, flower of Columba,
Flower of the Baptist
                    flower of the Intimate Sun, and You.

Century flower –

I see the whole journey from I to I am;
I see *the I is broken — the I dismembered —*
As all the myths say
                    and as Your Life said too

— to reach beyond the edge of all self-consciousness,
To go wide open into beauty and be there!

At the edge of a veil, like a membrane

                    stretched to the sky

Where it's You who comes through to me

                              and not I to You?

Oh Intimate Friend of the sky and the ground
God all around me
                    God within

You come to me whether I see You or not
You come to me in eyes, in the blessing of faces
You come in the light, and in the grass

And the cross that our directions make
Is the cross I'm sitting in,
Part of its centre —
Heart still out of breath from the climb

                              pumping blood

— the call nearby
                    of the invisible crake

A fly buzzing
                    even at this height

The mountain where Canon Watson died.

It would be a fine place to die:

Dun-ee, Dun I

This is the place
Where the I can go
Through the eye of the needle

that becomes the sky

Dun-ee, Dun I

Who built this cairn of stones,
Who piled it here to be seen —
With an egg-shaped one at its summit,
Where I look back to where you landed ...
Your coracle hauled ashore and buried,
Then your slow hour's walk up here ...

And the thousands who have walked here since.

Two white yachts down in front of the Abbey
Floating together

quietly as swans

And this rock the oldest rock in time,
This rock from the deep sea root

of the Old Earth

This Iona earth become New Earth

new again

In the dreamtime we're called to re-enter
To be in the dream as worship

To be in the dream as receivers

and *act* on the dream

To risk the dream between you and I —
Where You come in between you and I.

You are the star that comes between us

Star of inestimable form and colour

— the star I could not draw or name —

You that light between us
As You light the land with Your Sun

... far back towards the shores of granite
and the road we have come

far forward to the sea-mist haze of the horizon
and the future time

Dreaming horizon, the purple sail of a boat
That moved, huge for a moment, behind the Island
Then drifted across and disappeared ...

Unborn future, dreaming to be born

Unborn future, waiting to be seen

Unborn future coming between us
as the eagle drifts

Skin after skin and veil after veil
'And all he has left is his walking shadow
And his only reality is the sun.'

And as the sun throws my sitting shadow forward
At the peak of a triangle on the goldening grass

196

I see the sun I speak of you is You
And the shadow I am is all I was.

You have come into my heart now
Come into me wholly

O Lord fill me with Your Sun

Now the two swan-yachts float apart

They circle as I do
                    round this cairn of stone

– this beacon and this burial –

        but nothing is buried here, only the past.

The Spirit has never died in the sky;
The Spirit has never died in the ground –

Only flesh and blood are finished
And the sun in our blood
                    flows on for ever ...

River to ocean, and ocean to shore,
We flow out to You in love
                    and You return to us in Love.

We flow out to You in fire
                    and You return to us in Fire.

We flow out to You in air
                    and You return to us in Air –

                    in this buffeting wind!

And all Your names are One Name

   Your Kingdom one source of white rain-colour

      raining colour into form.

You Rainbow Worker, Rainbow-Dreamer,
That You should achieve through Creation
Total expression, total truth —

And we are the parts of that
Trying to find the other parts
However far we have wandered, and we have wandered far

And You give us all the time there is

   to make one journey of return

      the only journey there is, the journey home.

And now I give myself wholly over
Lying out face down on the ground ...
One by one, I see your faces in the sun
Emerging and dissolving back into light
Out of one face that becomes the sun —
A woman's face, with her hair all light
Like yours, that was the Face of Love

And so I dreamt the dream of surrender

              and I came down.

The Abbey bell tolling and echoing,
The gulls echoing it in their cry, answering it —
Winging in its sound, dim white to the gathering twilight,
As it peals at the pace of footsteps

           like the tick of a metronome

And like ours as we file quietly in to pray.

For ten minutes of silence, still the bell
Echoing into feeling ... where there are no words
And nothing to do but be, until you begin to speak
Leading the prayers, for the people you name, murmuring
Behind the hollow sound of wind through the microphone ...

God, in Your Mercy

HEAR OUR PRAYER

But in the spell the air hangs in
We know You hear us –
Even in the murmuring that escapes us
Like a child, muffled at a distance ...
In the leaning, breathing Body of Prayer we become
As we speak our own in our hearts:

May I come to stand
In the fullness of what I am
And may I have the courage to be
Whatever it is You want me to be ...

I meet you outside in the cloister, smiling
With the warmth of the day inside you.
We decide on the mountain, to see the sun set
The way it does in your eyes, with expectancy ...

You tell me the dream you had,
Your voice suddenly clear in the ringing air
As you share it, pronouncing each syllable –
Your dream of being born, and your fear of it,
Of being in a labour ward about to give birth,

The bedpans around you full of blood

                        and I hear you.

We glance up at the reddening sky as we begin to climb.

And who is being born, you or a child?
What is it you're afraid of giving birth to?
And what do you need, being pregnant now?
I wonder where the seeding is in earth and air
That makes the light in your eyes what it is
And the dream that grips you, inside your body
Where no hands are, and no one is –

Only this ease of walking between us
As we stand strangely upright in our height
And the space of our steps between us as we slow
Gravely, respectfully, royally apart –
Listening to each other, our movement like a dance.
You talk about singleness and difference
And not coming together *'until you know your own path'*.

You sit down on a rock, the sky behind you,
To tell me about the man you're with, and men;
I think of the Father I'm here with
And the man who said, *'I and the Father are one ...'*
And how we are *not one* until we find him:

May he find the rock in him
And know the earth is his Mother

On the rock I'm sitting on, the actual stone, beside you
As I glance down at your taut laced boots.

Then we stand and go to the height
We've climbed inside the heart, and climbed closer,
It reaching like a membrane around both of us,

A caul of reddening air we're breathing –

                and you see it

Rose on the horizon, woven in dove-grey cloud
Over the far down rippling silver mirror of the sea ...
It's the heart of the sun in the cloud

the heart woven in a swathe of silk
               with a hole at its centre –

Deepening down into our gaze as we wait,
Deepening down invisibly into our blood:
Blood royal, blood rose, rose charged with feeling
Where no words need to be
               as we turn to come down.

Rock-climbing in reverse,
Down the steepest way as if by chance!
The rocks and tussocks hold us all the way
Till we walk down the lane towards the Nunnery
And straight through its shadow – *straight through fear now* –

And you say simply, 'It's good you're here.'
I wonder for a moment what you mean,
In a flash as if my whole body is empty
And who I am is *all new and unknown to me.*

We sit outside the prefab pub, on a bench
With the war memorial of the world behind us
Looking out on the water of Martyrs Bay
Blue in the last light, reaching into the Sound.
As the moon rises to whiten the darkening, lapping waves
I tell you how the past has been my royal road
Weaving me into the depth of time and memory
In this one story where we've been all of it –
So I can no longer say I am apart from it;

I am in the weft and warp of its body

as you are.

And where does all this knowing bring us to?
Gentleness: awareness – patience and a rightness
Reaching to touch the side of your arm ...
I glance at you in profile, from the beginning
Seeing your shadowed face of suffering in the lightening air,
As you look up at the moon and sigh, *ha*, and I ask you,
'If you were the moon, how would you be?' 'Waxing.'
'Remind me, what way is that now?'
'Growing bigger!' 'Well, feel free –' and we laugh.

And down on the beach
There's a gathering round a blaze of crackling wood,
Faces lit up in its glow, the shot sparks rising,
As they play old sixties songs: Dylan and Don Maclean
Singing, '*I want to sta-nd in your heart.*'
We catch their laughter as the music strays
With its warm scent of gladness-fire, drawing us in;
Suddenly the beach could be somewhere in Greece
Where we are all still travellers under the stars.
As you tap your feet to the beat to dance

I glance out over the moonlit water,
And there's a light like a star coming to meet us,
Like in a small fishing boat, but you can't see it,
You can only see the light as it invisibly closens
White over the whispering, blackening swell ...

A star is coming across the water
She has come to guide my way ...

And we turn to stand and freely embrace.

I walk back in the dark to the cloister,
Pause to sit, gazing down at the stones —
And across all my doubts, fears and wonderings
A single white dove's feather drifts slowly past.

Day 19

Iona

What *is your name? What is your name*
In the dawn?

What was your name? I couldn't grasp it from the dream
As the voice and your presence

        slipped away.

Only you were with me in its syllables
And the sound of your name was beloved,
The suffix to your name was Beloved

        Magdalena.

You leaned by me, you reached towards me …

Who is the woman who comes in your dreams
And leaves you waking alone when she fades?
Sun outside now … she is the earth, calling.
The breakfast bell is ringing. She is Eve, too.
And she's the earth's shape of longing

        like you.

What is the sign now? Still the white feather
That the wind blows out of my black bag, up against the light …
Then floats down to the grass, where I bend to pick it up.

Where is it leading towards? St Michael, again.
I lift the latch and go inside –
Standing where the sun streams through the windows
As it becomes light, clear light, behind me eyes

        then a sun

Then a cross of light the sun is eclipsed by

And now there are faces, faces in the light,
Faces of the dead returning in procession,
Every kind of face, with one light about them,
One yellow-gold hue suffusing all their passing features.

There's a young girl's, turning into shadow
As her eyes become an animal's, like a cat's or an owl's
And she turns again, becoming radiant and lovely
Then a long road up a mountain
Lined with tall trees that are translucent
Then a gold window etched with a woman's shape in shadow
Her curves reversed out in the glass —
As it becomes a Celtic cross laced with gemstones
And then an old man as the window becomes fire

Revelation, imagination,
Light and shadow conjoining together,
Gold and the shadow saying *we become one*

                                        in the end.

Imagination: Your eye direct,
Your eye without intermediary, teaching me
Imagination — Creation, generosity.
How can we divine the depth of your colours,
Your purpose and your becoming?

                              But in ourselves
And in the dream where we are the whole of Your world.

And who am I? What are you going to call me?
Only your unknowing allows you to see me
Past the label you'd put on me — or I would on you
(As you put it, Helen, as we sit in the place where I sleep,
And I know what you mean, but I need to be alone;
I leave you taking off our labels like clothes ...)

Outside on the grass I'm back with you, Columba,
Finding exhausted on the shore a white crane
You charged a brother to look after, for three whole days,
Until it rose into the sky, knowing its way home ...
I think of the saving sign you made over everything
And how the more you loved, you'd know at a distance
When she cried out in labour and called your name;
How you withdrew then to be alone;
How you raged at any injustice like a king;
And how the shadow of that king was in you, too,
Before the long lonely climb
                              to your purity began:
On the Hill of the Angels, where they surrounded you
In the blinding light of your hut as the peeping monk bent,
And in the four years you had to live on, surrendered,
Broken and bound and humbled to earth,
Before you hurried alone to the altar to die –
And the peace that infused your dying face with joy
Before a storm came that no one could calm
And the darkness of the raiding Viking centuries fell

        blackening the light like a sky,

Blackening the grass and bloodying the sand ...

As the sheep bleat flocking out to pasture
A sparrow comes and carries the feather away in his mouth.

Black sky, and blue, as I walk down.
Black sky, and blue, as I find you, Rick,
Outside the dark-blue-painted hotel,
Lying on the grass with your raven hair
And bare tanned arms,
The sun beating down on every detail of your face.
I ask how long you've been here – months ...
And how long you're staying – *'for as long as it takes'*.

You've got no agenda, just to be here
Loving the gathering of souls, but not the Abbey.
There's another Iona for you:
Beach parties, rapping with joints, and rituals.
So what's changed? It's all in the bridging now

Where Pagan and Christian meet and let go
Because we're each holding the shadow;
And there's more, there's one thing between us now
That can't wait any longer – this beautiful earth
And the Dream of Life while there's still time –
Which means we're here to complete one another: Your plan
Beyond all our difference and imagining.
I say, 'We're like seed men with seeds in our pockets,
Scattering them at every opportunity.' You nod
And your black hair deepens my brightness
As my brightness lightens yours; still sad – you tell me
About the water elemental you saw on the north shore
With her gull wings and message of grief,
Woven into the water of your seeing as she stood
And told you she couldn't stay and that it might be too late.

And on the sand you drew it –
'You draw, you write, you dream on the sand
Then the tide comes in and washes it away, and it's done.'
It's over for then, as then is now, each time –
And it's all transient; your words score the air,
Your hand gesturing to the ends of your fingers,
And it's your whole body, given into the picture
Playing on the sand ... and you're saying,
'It's transient art' – the whole thing, transient –
When we see there is no separation *and it's all Yours.*
How did you see that? How did you come to it?
You *fell* – you fell near the spouting cave,
So you were hanging off a ledge of rock –
And when you came to you knew you'd nearly gone.

Then you were young for the world, as you are.
You ask if I've seen the Well of Eternal Youth.
'On the mountain?' 'Yeah.' 'Haven't seen it –'
'Well, I'll take you there'
                              – as we stand to walk.

On the way past the Nunnery in the sun, you pause
To show me Sheela na Gig high in the wall
Above a cleft of bare window embedded in the stone
Which she spans, worn to hand-smoothed white
As if birthing the whole of the world like a cloud
Pregnant with all we have denied her: her face like a nun's.

As we walk, the waves break on in my being,
Echoing what you've said ... *to be like flowers in the sun,*
Yellow with light and scent, where the page is the real ground,
The feeling, the living air, and the sea the real sea.
I tell you about the whale out beyond the north shore,
As you told me, Val
                         how he circled the boat,
Came up out of the grey glittering water, near Staffa,
And danced for the boat, circling around it, dancing!

You, Val, and all the others on the boat gone still,
All of you gone silent unable to say anything,
And afterwards, as he sank, and the moment held ...
Feeling the need to just hold one another ...
So strong was the healing that came across the water

Where he swims now, deep-diving invisibly.

You take me over the top of the hill,
Over and down, to an outcrop of rock
Where the ground deepens under the grass, out of sight,
And the water opens under its dry face, a pool
Shaped like a triangle of water in the green ...

208

A pubis of water, where you bend – 'Here she is' –
A pubis of water with light brown stones in it
Laced with delicate weed-fronds like hair,
Where you cup your palm and drink from it; I follow
And the water tastes like wine
                        soft brown communion wine,

Soft brown as your hidden eyes
                                in the light.

We sit for a while quietly, then you leave me,
Raising your hand and smiling
As you go back up, and the mountain takes you
Over its shoulder and its rim as I lean back under my eyes.

To be new again ... to be a child,
To know what we knew then was real and true,
And to look at the earth now and say *it is time*
As the planets line up with Pluto
                                to come through or die

To come through the eye, this gateway of the dying.
I think of those who come near death
And find it is the dying-through-being-born-through
One passage, one movement ... one and the same:
Well of Eternal Youth, be with us now.

To feel that, to seed it, to go out and spread it,
Mentioning something here, suggesting something there,
Strange ministry for strange days, all of ours to share
Outside of any church, whatever our names are ...
And how define it? By what makes your heart sing,
The song that must be sung for the living,
No throwaway tune or line – so call it fire;
To realise this is the poem, and we're writing it,
And that is the veil we pass through

the veil of the mind

The veil that makes it *only words on a page*
Until we come through to the thing itself, the living thing,
The only ground of You there is, Living God.

Sitting up, cross-legged,
The water beckoning as I move beside it
To dream the second dream with my eyes awake:

Baptise me here in the well
As I stand in the water, naked
I kneel in the water, naked
As the well deepens

Until I'm swimming inside of it.

I breathe, I breathe up air around me
I swim the wave

Letting the wave break over me ...

Then we stand in the well together.

I draw a saving sign on your forehead
As you answer me with one on mine.

We stand in the well together, dripping water
Holding hands loosely, facing one another

We stand in the well together
And pour the water's libation over each other ...

And you with your tanned skin and close-cut hair
Your eyes the colour of the well
Your mouth tasting of the well, kissed.

We are one

        then the well deepens.

Two people descend, and the well becomes a circle
Two people descend, and the well becomes an eye

And in the circle of the eye

        a star is shining.

Is it a star or is it the moon?
It's too far away to tell
Deep into the eye, deep into the soul

And deep in gold light, somewhere far under
Christ's face is a young girl's
The procession is walking, walking upwards
And they are walking to the well.

Deep in the well-light

        women abandon themselves to the wave

Women naked

        women in their full exotic beauty …

And out of the well, out of them all
Comes the Magdalene
        the Magdalene of Now.

And I come down
        with you inside me, by the bell.

I sit by you, Helen, at supper.
The sunlight shining luminous on to your face …

You talk about being in prison in Stirling and how the women
Took you under their wing there, as only women can.
I think of what it means to stand for what we believe,
And it's love, not anger, shining in your skin,
And it is the sun, but not the sunlight alone
Or your fire that gave you the strength to go through with it,
And I glance into the grey-blue of your eyes.

We walk outside to sit on the grass
 – Donald, Jenny, Val – to discuss tomorrow night.
I hear the first notes of the violin
As we pass the door where you're rehearsing.
It echoes when I walk down again to call you,
Drawing me to something I can't yet name,
A feeling free on the air, given before time.
You talk about the sadness of the earth down the line
Where the static crackles … a bedrock of grief
As you feel it in parallel, and when I walk back by the music door

All the sadness in the world is woven in those strings
As the bow sings, smoothing them, soothing them
Like fine rain falling, nameless feeling
From a heart open that has no words to speak but song,
And nothing to solace it but song
The way a bird would sing, but deeper, sadder
Than any bird is when you see it is a ruin

A ruin of broken stones, where the wind sings
As I walk to St Mary's, where the pilgrims rested,
Down the branch of an old street covered in grass now,
Love among the ruins, as I glance at the Abbey roof,
Gaze out on the deep peace of the blue-jewelled water,
The herd nosing by the fence, and the gulls in the light
Like flicking white sparks of flame –

                    the Ross sheathed in the heat-mist

And what these stones have broken open to:
My house, a house of stone broken open to beauty,
Sadness-beauty

            that the Dream is ...

We walk in through the door to your service
And I see what you've been making all afternoon
On the nave floor, in the centre among the flagstones:
A huge spiral woven in sand, with stones and shells
And seaweed lacing, white-yellow, luminous on the grey,
And a stone you give to each one of us as we come in ...
Wondering at it in the flickering light, wide-eyed,
Smiling in the quietness and the quiet it brings
As your hands move tracing its outline filled in,
Inwards and inwards to the centre that is *She*

Our eyes still transfixed when we sing 'Ubi Caritas'
Then 'Veni Creator Spiritus' ... as you lead us
And in the chant, as the words hang, the whole air's attuned,
Warmed through as we warm it

                  and the Song comes down

 – it comes around our shoulders in the falling light
As we ask You to be with us and speak your name
Looming cloud-like across a mountain ...

Before you spell the Seven Days of Creation
You call a labour of love as if it could be anything less

AND IT WAS VERY GOOD

The waters were broken, a cradle made ready;
Rhythm was established

             and you know

IT WAS VERY GOOD ...

– how could we ever have doubted it?
What did you tell us with your gloomy half-truth
About Genesis made like a punishment for children

... when we see that it is Her who made it too?

And all creatures as we are, we raise the roof
With an old song of fire that blisters the light
Thrown up like gold dust out of our hands!

'All creatures of our God and King ...'

But wait
        listen
              look

– the whale is real, and the whale is calling us
As you speak it from the Psalms:

There go the ships,
There is that Leviathan that thou has made to play therein

He lifts his head, her head out of the water,
Knowing she is alone and that the sunlit sea is empty.
She flicks her enormous black gleaming tail,
Showering the air around her with flung silver drops ...
                               as we sing

'Veni Cre-a-tor Spi-ri-tus'

And you stand and speak of the sea we are in
Rippling outwards from our listening grey eyes

Strange islands and resounding rivers
The whispering of love and the dream
The tranquil night at the time of rising dawn ...

214

Silent music, sounding solitude
The supper that refreshes and deepens life

– and it comes from the other side of the waves
Where the voice is free, and breath and being are free
To feel the fullness of all you give
In the Name of Love
                that is life as it takes us …

Long silence. Then we sing again

'*Veni Cre-ator Spi-ritus*'

– as the whale dips out of sight, leaving the waves
That cover her traces
                leaving no trace
As she moves in her length like an invisible shadow

And you speak of God's strength
That *'fixed the earth on its foundation for ever'*
Up hill, down dale, rivers – canyons – fjords, the open sea:
Creator, coagulating the earth out of Your Body –
That is ours too … that the whale is calling us to

        that You infused yourself into

        cell by compassionate cell

… as we return our pebbles one by one
                exchanging them for shells …

The violin echoing its adagio

And how can we be blind to it? How can we go on
Living the lie the earth is ours to destroy?

Your words were simple, and they shame us to hear them
When all you were doing is writing a letter:

'How can we buy or sell the sky?'

'Every part of this earth is sacred to our people ...'

'Our dead never forget this beautiful earth'

'The rivers are our brothers and sisters ...'

'And if we sell you land ...' as you must have known,
As your quill scratched the words on the page,
Earth-Christ in your crown of feathers,
Did you see the tragedy we are harvesting now?

How come all is broken-hearted?
Is it the only way justice can become peace?
Is it the only way we can enter Your body,
Your body of broken bones it is ours to redeem?

There is another way, if we choose it.
The Judgement's our own, over our heads
— *ours* not Yours!

                    Yours is Love

          God of Ages, Leviathan Love.

                    Creation.

The spiral waits. The spiral stays
Like an eye of mercy folded deep in the storm
And in your last prayer you name the whale
At the still centre, at the spiral's hub,
And all that is left here is stillness

The violin softly, lingeringly breaks
As I stay where I am, unable to move; you too,
As it plays on above the scraping chairs
Into the stillness, becoming the stillness,
The vanishing course where everything's waiting
As I wait for you, watching her play, by the door.

We follow our steps back to the bar
And stand in the crowded light under the packed ceiling,
But another part of us is walking without saying anything
Where the stillness stays, and we walk on past,
On past the bench and the charred sticks in the dark,
On down the lane before we cross to the sand
And all I can feel is your breathing beside me:

The wind so still – the wind's dropped
And the lights from the houses are still in the water
And the sand is like sand on another planet,
Alive with jumping sandhoppers, like the finest rain
Where no rain was, not a breath, nothing –
Only our own, sitting now
                              with the sky, waiting;

The sky was waiting, the whole sky was waiting
Far up into the glittering stars above our heads,
The sky waiting, and the earth, the sea waiting,
And as we gaze it's as if the sky is going to speak,
Then the stars; the stars themselves are waiting

And I can feel the blood tingling in my hand

And the slightest touch as I reached for your hand
Was so cool and clear it was like dew on fire;
It was so still I could barely bear to touch you
As we lay back then, we lay there in silence

We lay like dancers, stranded

                landed

We lay like dancers on an unknown planet
And when we sat and faced each other it was in crystal
In the cool moon-dark, the cool moon-sand-dark

And when we touched each other's lips they were sealed
Silent to the touch of my finger on mine
And on yours, and on mine again

                soror mystica

Because it was the star we were under, and we knew
The star, and the moon – the moon you'd asked for –
And it was the patience of God and the silence beyond peace.

Day 20

Iona

A brightness like a silver blaze behind my eyes
As I see us still there on the sand.

It was the star we sat in
the prayer of the star

– touching forehead to forehead.

It was the white feather come drifting down

falling invisibly from the sky

'Mind that which is pure in one another ...'

Echoing in me inwardly
calling me alone

And it's the most delicate balance between both of us.

Now let the wind flow, let the Word flow
As I walk on to the grass asking for a sign ...
And in the Chapel there it is:

a butterfly, lit up, flapping at the window

Above the open Book and unlit taper candle,
Saying *let me out, let me free, this is the time.*

This morning's your holiday; you've taken it off.
I chop away at the onions, longing to get through –
Then as I turn for a moment a young woman

With long deep gold hair wearing an apron
Is walking through the kitchen; we all glance up
And I ask you who she is

                'Oh, that's Magdalena …'

And as our eyes briefly meet
Her silence is a soft glow around my heart
Leaving the light streaming through the windows.

You meet me outside in the cloister
With bare arms, a blue T shirt, and shorts.
We sit near the sculpture base, poring over the map
Of the Island spread flat, floating in aquamarine.
We try to decide where to go: 'St Martin's Cove?'
'The bay is beautiful there.' 'Let's see where it takes us.'
We leave the Abbey behind, then the Nunnery,
Branching left on to a farm lane crossing between fields …
You breathe out, stretching your arms in the sun,
Light and easy in your step, and I say

'Last night was the star. Today's the wilderness …'
And the open ground of the Machair closens towards us.

There's a cow and her calf, and wild flowers
Lacing the long grass all along the verge
So clear in the light, the blue all around us
Blending with the light and the air as you name them.
We come to a field where all the cattle are asleep
Either side of a gap – and you see their patience,
One laying her muzzle in front of her on the ground.
And as I glance down – there in the grass
Is the outline of a cross gouged open in the sand,
A cross of uncut stone like a wound among the daisies.

We walk on where the ground opens the grass to sand, to sea,
Up a long stony path your words fall to,

With the stone of the centuries under our feet
And the stone of the monks of 563 ... the same stones;
I glimpse one in a girdle carrying a pail for water,
Dissolving into the light as we reach the top

Of a rock where the ground opens down, the loch
Spreads like wings of water, fenced round its edges,
And you tell me it's the Island's only water supply ...
– Loch Stonaig, slate stone-blue, Iona-sized.
We closen and stand for a moment by its stillness.
We ask that its sanctuary of water be guarded
Free of harm, free like the last water;

                        imagine:

Look at what your eyes can see
And then see into it and you will find the Dream

We check the map again, divining
Where there's no path now, only rough grass
As we come downhill, following the rift
With the Hill of the Lambs over our shoulders,
Looking for sundew – 'Yes, they're tiny' –
Combing the length of the marshy grass with our eyes.
Sundew: hidden flowers of the moist gold light

            in the moist crack of the ground.

And reaching the bay, the Hollow of the Big Mouth,
Walking on to the pebbles at the water's edge
Where the waves lap in, leaving the small white surf
As they suck back ... we look down at our feet:
They glow wet with the light on them;
We've stumbled on a jeweller's paradise for free
– pearl, pink, beige, black, brown, and red,
Green-black, green-grey, tan, and ochre –

All the shades you can think of; in such rich abundance
We turn them up, beachcombing like children ...

I couldn't name the rock, or the colours beyond name.
We crouch to them in wonder – and as
You stood up your eyes shone and the blue of your shirt
With the gold of the sun completed them

   Rainbow, rainbow of light
            where the rainbow splashed in the ground

Colour driven into stone
            polished by the tongue of the sea ...

And is this what it means to be free to love?
How else can we see, how else can we breathe
The breadth of Your being all around us?

So you ask me, and all I can answer is this given moment
Without words, only eyes, as you closen
In the moment before you speak –

Love, given in feeling between us like the dream,
Love, if we can open beyond all it is *not*
That means you're standing where you're standing
Holding its gift in your hands and pockets as I am
And your eyes darken, darker brown, wondering.

We round towards where the Cave should be
Somewhere over the edge, down among these rocks
In a Baie-blue inlet of sunlit, aquamarine water
Chequered light and dark with shadows like clouds ...
But we can't find it – and we appear to be lost,
We're heading off-piste
                        and down into a cleft, still looking

Before we sit down and give up.

The cliff high behind us and no ground between us
So we could neither sit nor lie at a distance
And it was there I found you, and it was earth between us
Clothed as we were, and it made no difference –
We didn't even need to touch each other to feel it;
It was *earth* in the embrace of you against the rock
And it was Her between us as we lay there
And it was you, Magdalene, in the depth of your eyes,
The earth in you, woman, as it came alive.
I said, 'Don't forget, we're dancing,' and we were
And laughing too, because it was innocent.
We closed our eyes silently and offered it up

And in the end, I said, 'We'll offer each other up.'

We didn't stumble or fall as we walked,
We danced – and the sun kept shining
And nobody saw us or whispered *thou shalt not.*
The hidden cleft was itself, and not what it was not,
And no touch or word or kiss was what it was not.

We let it go then and spoke of other things.
Then we retraced our steps, into the beginning ...

The blue is all around us, and this is Love's Island,
Iona of my heart, and of the New Dispensation.

You leave me to the mountain,
To go over to the Well to rest and give thanks;
But then what is it that falls over the other side?
What is it that slowly gathers and weighs
Like a grief or sadness I cannot name
As I watch two black butterflies cavorting over the edge

Over the ragged broken wire,
And over the Dark Strath towards Calf Island?

What is the inverse, the other side of blue,
That falls and has to fall as high as it rises
Holding height and depth equally in the scales
It keeps adjusting, weighing, and then lightening?
There's a centre here I have not reached.
There's a place I have not found
To glide like a gull

                in equipoise.

No: You reach us up as You reach us down,
Reminding us always how of the earth we are,
Or say my heart is always one step ahead of me
Showing my true way, drawing in and back,
Over the broken wire of freedom, from the edge
Where I don't presume to go.

                Ah Lucifer, old friend

Bright one, eternal puer,
Fallen angel of light or pride,
You never quite leave us alone.
And You are for the heart that must always go deeper
And so you balance me in sadness on the wind.

The bell goes – and I've missed the service.
But I don't really want to speak to or see anyone.
You have taken me apart in the wind.

But when I come down and meet you, Val,
Before we head to the Coffee House for the reading,
And we walk down to the bar to catch a quick Guinness,
What is this gulf like an abyss
That leaves you wanting to say *oh mercy*
And drinks the black draught like a river of sleep?

You know it, dying *and how the dying is the rising*,
And I forget it, so it's as pure a dark
As the light was bright in front of my face,
But I can't see my face for the blackness streaming
Or the glass.

While we wait and the space slowly fills
You all arrive. I improvise an order
And it's more like chaos. What are we doing here?
The chairs scuffle with the focus off-centre.
What is it that slowly calms the air,
Coagulating listening into gradual stillness,
Stillness and then warmth, gathering, beating?
I know it has nothing to do with me now,
Except in giving and holding this space:
I give myself for the thing to happen – it does
And, as it happens, it happens to be all of us

All of us; as you recite 'The Journey of the Magi'
Your old face lights up like a boy reading Hopkins,
Then you undercut it all with your 'sly witty rhymes',
Elizabeth, and the whole place explodes in laughter,
Relaxing everything as you turn and smile.
You enchant us with your shy poems about children,
And it's your first time reading, as you speak a haiku,
Clearing your throat in the middle, then again;
Then you lull us back to life with blues from Glasgow,
Your clear singing voice fills under the ceiling ...

And who is to say what's real and what's not?
Who is to say what's *good* from an armchair
When an eighty-four-year-old can flatten us all?
I lose you all in God, find you as I'm found
As *one* of you, reading the Psalms or mending a fence.
It's all the work we do, and it's all good.
And the draught of the good wind blows over the candles.

Praise be to the Human Song, alleluia.
Praise be to Your inviolate weave of grief and laughter.

We walk outside in the dark; you say, 'You seem taller,'
And it's with the lightening and the letting go
Where I learn to lose myself and relinquish control,
As the wind blows round, fresh on our faces
And I don't know what You want, but I'm halfway in you
In the mystery where I lose me and find You;
I am a blank space for You, like my shadow in the night.

When you mention the prayers for tomorrow morning
We decide to go inside to try to write them together
In the Chapter House where I'm sleeping rough,
The mattress leaning up against the wall,
And the long table where we light two candles,
One for each, brother and sister.
Is this what it means to be together?

The wind gales on outside as we listen
Side by side, going in, attuning
So I'm only aware of the wind and your shadow;
And suddenly there are lines, lines in the quiet,
Words in the quiet, inside the wind
In the quiet inside your eyes that can hear,
Seeing them whispering under the nib of your pen

And in minutes, a moment it seems, they are done.
We turn to each other in the flickering light.
I see you, sister; I see you as you are.
I see what we're here for in the Body of Love,
The body of blue and black air that's dreaming us
Where the wind blows all reality between us,
All reality that is prayer, in your candlelit eyes
When prayer goes free and all speech is open:

LORD OF THE RAINBOW
LORD OF ALL IMAGINABLE COLOURS
YOU ARE THE LIGHT AND SHADE IN EVERYTHING
YOU ARE THE CIRCLE AND CENTRE OF OUR TURNING WORLD
MAY WE COME TO SEE IN ALL THINGS
THE FULLNESS OF YOUR REALITY
AND MAY WE COME TO SEE THROUGH EACH OTHER
THE FULLNESS OF OURSELVES IN YOU.

And in your hand:

'It can be through failing that we come close to you
As you reach into our hearts with Your healing power ...'

The door lies open to the wind: we go out,
I walk with you a while, then alone

                              exultant in its breath

Where I lose your outline as I lose mine –

Until there's only the Abbey as I come back, timeless.

Day 21

Iona

T he spacious firmament on high
  With all the blue ethereal sky
  And spangled heaven and shining frame
Their great original proclaim

— so we sing, and the words hang still,
Lifting to the roof in their clarity

                              into the blue

In the silence before our voices return
And I jot them down ... *how long have we known this?*

'And the light of the world is a joy and a blessing.'
It echoes in our open hearts in gentleness ...
As we sing as a Body of Light now, a soft Lamb Body,
The sun streaming through in all-feeling behind our eyes.

Asking for Your help, we say again

AND MAY THE SPRIT OF YOUR FREEDOM SUSTAIN US

              the sunlight   the blue

          the Light this whole building

                              breaks open to

You reading the prayers in your soft clarity,
Your head quietly bowed as every word touches through

— *and we will not offer You offerings that cost us nothing* ...

as the piano follows us out.

And this is the Pilgrimage day, our day.
We gather at the foot of St Martin's Cross
Where you stand in blue with your shepherd's crook and bag,
Ali, and the wind blows back the forelock of your hair,
Your red hair, like a Mohican, as you speak above our heads,
Your bare legs and feet braided into sandals,
And you point to the knotwork tracery, all interweaved
– as we all are, standing here – with the whole of life.
This All of Life and awe your faces radiates
As you say lightly at the top of your voice into the wind

Bless to us O God the earth beneath our feet
Bless to us O God the path whereon we go
Bless to us O God the people that we meet

We begin to wind slowly down the path
– the path we walked alone, hours before –

                                        where you lead us

And I'm walking with you, Magdalena,
In your corduroy skirt, braces, brown tights,
White sweater; your hair tied back in a bunch.
You turn to me and smile in your soft gold light,
Saying hello in your hesitant Czech English,
And in the smiling pause before I speak
All I can see is the silence and depth in your eyes,
Unshielded from the sun – and the curve of your mouth,
Magdalen, and your thick lustrous hair
                          not black or light, but gold now

As you talk about the church in your country,
The younger ones, and the new Protestant movement
That is for all people, beyond hierarchy ...
All war-torn people in the suffering in your eyes

As you tell me about Prague – your city –

And even when Rosemary gently buts in,
Wanting to talk about the Beguines and Matthew Fox,
All I can hear is your silence –
All I can feel is your patient presence
In the honey-coloured light like a glow around you
(Confess: I'm only talking to be near you).

We fall silent together by this rising path of stones,
The Purgatory Path, I drop a few yards behind,
And you go on with the patience of the ages inside,
Glancing down at your feet among the stones
As you tread and step around them, unconcerned,
Knowing who you are – and You?
You have buried your secret so deep in her
She will never need to prove it or speak it aloud;
She is it, your loving daughter.

Coming to the top, we stand on the rock,
Chatting as we slowly crocodile to join you …
The sun beating down on the stones, the heat rising
As we walk down together towards the loch.

There we gather, by its clear Body of Water,
Its surface skimmed to the slightest of breezes,
And you ask again, raising your glad Scots face:

Bless to me O God my soul that comes from on high
Bless to me O God my body that is of earth
Bless to me O God each thing my eye sees
Bless to me O God each thing my ears hear
Bless to me each odour that goes to my nostrils,
Bless to me each taste that goes to my lips
Each note that goes to my song
Each ray that guides my way

Then you turn, begin to lead us downwards
Over the heather grass, towards the Marble Quarry ...

And as we walk, there's you, Val, in your kerchief
Tied around your head against the sun – and with her
You fall silently into step like sisters,
Sisters in suffering and mercy
                    your faces bowed in the heat

Leaving me some distance behind, seeing you.
We cross a narrow path of planks and beams over the bog,
One by one, eyes down to our feet –

And when we glance up, the black and white collie sheepdog,
With his brush of a tail and panting glad tongue,
Is rounding us up, racing back and forth from behind,
Like we're sheep! *His sheep* – he streaks ahead and back.
Laughter when you say, 'He's got the job.'

We come down to an outcrop where the path leads down;
He waits on his forepaws – and you snake ahead,
In all your colours, with your bare arms, legs, and heads
Swaying as the sea-sky opens on the down horizon
Above the rocks, swaying in the heat of the rhythm,
Silently, as the movement breathes through us
And we follow, marching into translucency,
Not armoured now, but naked in peace,

Reaching down among the rocks and the sea
Where the waves wash in and the cliffs rise sheer:
White stones, huge white boulders lying everywhere –
One of them whale-sized, flecked in wet seaweed-green,
White as the air, and the surf breaking in ...
And the rusted cutting frame from eighty years ago
Stranded like an old tramcar without an engine,
Rotting as you gather round it, then we wander

Out to where the rocks rise above the water –
And you cross a slippery channel of sheer white marble
Between pauses of the rushing water sliding in
                                        as you climb.

You climb on to the rock with the sky white behind you,
Glancing into the air as if into a mirror,
And loosen your hair so it falls all round your shoulders,
Golden down your back, as you crouch and then kneel,
Smiling to yourself, as the sea breaks in, in,
Till there's only you and the rock and the rushing white swell
And behind us a voice begins to sing 'Rock of Ages'.

You come slowly down in your own time, like a queen,
And we retrace our steps, winding slowly back up.

We trek along in the sun towards Columba's Bay,
Back the way we came, circling the height.
From somewhere the echo of the Kyrie we sang
Plays on behind me, or ahead of me in the heat ...
Then from nowhere but inside my own listening heart
As I walk alone, where everything falls away to feeling
And it is not your face or form, or mine –
But this *being within each other* as I let you go,
That is You between us
                        and every face I can think of

As I open to you all, as you would want me to
Smiling to yourself, the light spreading from you
Reaching over all of us as I glance at you, moving
Walking in one light and love before we say anything

We closen down over the plain of grass
With its coracle mound by the edge where no coracle was,
Only the earth already greeting you, with a sign:
I see the True Man and the False Man on either side

That the bay divides into, and what it means to choose
Left or right, to see and be and walk that way,
Left and right, and both are here
                              where the sea embraces them.

And as we come down on to the sand by the mound
Where the grass breaks into pebbles
A cow is sitting with her forelegs tucked and tail spread out,
Whitened with a single patch of brown round her neck,
Like the white patience of ages, blinking, unconcerned,
And barely turning her head as we swarm around her
Wandering by the water and needing to sit down.

It is in these little acts of kindness – Dorothy,
Seeing my hunger as I finish the last of the water,
You manifest a bag of nuts and offer them round –
And miraculously or not there are enough, so you feed us
As the bag goes gratefully from hand to hand …
And you, Elizabeth, chime in, entertaining us:
'I'm going to be a hundred – only fourteen years to go.
Other people get there without trying, but I'm trying!'
Your brassy voice ringing on the air as we laugh,
Gazing at your fearlessness, and you remind us,
'That black cow when we first arrived did that cowpat here.
She said, "That's what I think of you!"' and we roar,
The tears coming to our eyes; the sky rolls
Over the grass as you hang on weakly to your sides –

And something of it spreads as we start to walk back,
Infectious as your levelling echo, Old Mother.
I see you ahead faltering in the heat, Josephine,
Weighed down with your bag as you step up to climb,
Saying nothing, uncomplaining, asking for nothing,
Just so suddenly and vulnerably here. I catch you up,
Lift it from you, and, slowing with you, hold your arm …
It's in these moments that You come –

Or else *'What good am I?'* as you sang it, Dylan.
What am I seeing? What am I actually doing?
And what is it that moves me that is no longer me?
And is? You turn and give me the mirror of your eyes,
Graciously thanking me as I linger a few steps with you
To thank you, silently, for letting me be this

And the little ones, too, as she leads them –
Both with their bare legs and beach shoes, as they follow,
One in her green shorts, the other in her white skirt
With her blond hair falling over her little red rucksack,
Too hot to talk, too free to complain –
'And a little child shall lead you ...' over the brow

Till we reach the path of stones leading down
All the way to the curve of sand where the cows lie
Amazing on their outrageous pasture, brown in the white glare.
We walk past them ... saying *this is our Kingdom*,
You saying it to them, free to wander, unconstrained:
You are sacred milk – go where you will ...

And so we come down on to the plain
                              by the Hill of the Angels,
Where the lunch waits out the back of the blue van:
I pause at the top for a moment, looking down
As you gather round it queuing, then sit at the hill's foot,
Spreading yourselves, talking, and the gulls hover over its brow,
Wings stretched wheeling, crying, waiting for scraps;
The girls sitting halfway up in a row, chatting –
The boys playing catch with an orange tossed in the air –
You queuing for tea, too thirsty to think –
You standing barefoot, resting your feet –
You looking over the map as you eat – and you leaning
Gazing, dreaming against the side of the van on a pair of stilts;

And were we waiting for you, isn't this how it would have been?
Isn't this exactly how it would have been, and is?
Out here in the open where the grass spreads like a carpet
Into the sea, and the sky rises, where You come –
As you come now, into this peace picnic in the sun ...
I look and look again, loving all of you, all of us
In all our ordinariness in every direction and dimension –

    as you stand now, smiling round

        and we finally stir to move on ...

And now I'm walking with you, Liz, as you talk
About teaching poetry to kids in school –
And how what matters *is the feeling, not the words,*
Or not the words first; if you can embody that,
If you can feel the poem inside you, then they can,
You're saying, and I add, 'That's what writing one is,
Or being one before you write it, you know' – like this

As we pause by a stile in a wire fence.
You leg it over first, Ali, while he waits patiently behind
And when you turn and lift him over in your arms
He lies there, with his eyes all trust, like a child's,
As we watch you smoothing his ears and then put him down,
Smiling in the glow of you where the love is so palpable.

And in the glow where the heat haze reaches the sky
We go up into a narrow rocky gorge, climbing ...
The heat beats down and we walk, still close in line –
And I don't know when it is, or where it is – where we are –
But suddenly, when I turn in the light, I see you, all –
I see you for a moment reaching far back over your heads,
Far back to the sea's edge and the sky lost in white,
As you walk in the light, and the light becomes the glory,
Your Glory in the sun where our faces are bright with it,

Walking in the heat, transparent in the light,
Thirsty in the heat, walking in slow motion ...
So slow for a moment you all seem to stop –
And the picture goes soundless, held like this for ever,
As you walk with your eyes closed in mid-step
And you follow with your sweater over your arm,
You follow with your head bowed in a white hat,
You look down in your dark glasses and baseball cap

And we are the People of God in the silence
In the held frame as the light streams through us
And the hairdresser from Glasgow, the Bahá'i from Wales,
And the fundamentalist from Bigglesthwaite are one,
One in the light reaching beyond all of us, in us
Where there are no words, only its breathing through us
In the blaze of what it is – *Glory, Glory* –
So brief you can barely see it –
So enormous as it stretches that we are all humanity:
Gone from ourselves into You and into this

        flash of gold awakening

     where you know ·

     you see with your light-struck eyes

   and you know

– and the *Halle, Halle, Halle-lu-ja* we sang is real
As real as the sun you saw as a host of heavenly angels,
And there is only one thing realer – this silence,
Or else the whole of the silence is singing, singing light,
And we are the singing light of the Song

     we are the Song

Gloria!
Gloria!
Gloria!

We are the People of God and the People of Desire.
We are the People of the Seeding and the People of Nakedness.
We are the People of the Streaming Light we live by

GLORIA

O Lord, let it come —

as we come down ...

We come down on the spreading grass, Dun I ahead of us
Dwarfing us as we descend from far back, in miniature;
The earth takes us into the curves of its lowering folds
As we come down looking for sundew, towards your Cell,
Its ring of broken stones, half hidden where it was,
Quietening your German voice, and everything hushes ...
We stand, and you can feel it deep in the ground.
We come to its centre, and you pause and say

Christ be before me, Christ behind me
Christ be above me, Christ beneath me
Christ be beside me, Christ within me,
Light of my heart —

And it's all heart, yours or mine,
This heart of light as we gaze down at the ground,
This heart of quiet it all goes inward to,
This hearts of hearts that is silence before sound.

And now we're for the mountain.

Taking the back route up, we wind and climb
Where the gorge of the Querns opens out like hands
Of smooth grey rock either side where we've come through

To the plateau – with the sun of the sky behind us
As we wander at the foot of it, each finding our way;
You lead up the left side, up Mary's Fank,
The woman's way up – you lead, and we take ourselves,
We spread out, and the mountain is crowning us
With the silence of what it individually means
To be alone with You, as we are.
I walk the far edge where the railing is the sea
Falling away to air where there's nothing to hold me,
Feet and elbows bent, balancing each step,
And the breath I breathe as I raise my head

      to the place that gives me breath

    behind my eyes, and I sit ...

    blue, over the lip ...
             and I see it.

You stand there, your blue shirt flapping in the wind
With a sad man in a deerstalker beside you,
A crucifix round his neck, outside his anorak,
Lamenting the English Church:
'They seem to have given up religion altogether.'
But you can see in his eyes, as I can,
That he has nothing but his own death to offer
As he stands, grey beside you, grey beside your blue,
Fully clothed beside your bare arms and sandalled calves,
And you glance down over the edge to the sea ...
Crucifixion and resurrection standing side by side
In the mystery, yet unable to meet –
Where the blue of the air
             is like a blade between you

And all you say that stays with me
Is that the light we find on the mountain

238

Is the light we have to bring down …
Not tablets of stone, but light now

Light at all our edges, and from our depth
Where the light of our bodies blends with the air
And All Creation, in the care of us

 – with the wind that is the light's strength around your throat,
The whole of your being vibrating with life.

Peace between nations
Peace between neighbours
Peace between lovers
In the love and God of Life

Peace between person and person
Peace between wife and husband
Peace between parent and child
The Peace of Christ above all peace

Bless O Christ our faces
Bless our faces, bless everything
Bless O Christ our eyes
Let our eyes bless all they see …

and in your eyes it is the light we bring down.
You turn and let the words go to the sky that gave them
And to our eyes' seeing
                              like seeds

As you lay your cloak of air into their dissolving,
Your cloak of love and your staff –
For us to choose to be.

We head down the way I've come,
Down among the rocks and lush tufts to the lane

We spread on to as the afternoon world greets us
And we fall into returning line – with one thing left to do.

Passing the Abbey at the edge of the old street of death,
Filing in under the arch of the oldest building
They built for burial, in the grey cool light
We come into its spell out of the sun: St Oran's
With its stone-carved hearth and simple silver cross
And bare flagstones we cover as we all sit together
Breathing in the cool air after the heat, into our skin,
While you speak of being *in the midst of death* as a beginning –
The graveyard where they buried pilgrims and kings
Where we're like ash floating in the breeze ...
Where we will return into the silence beyond form
Or shape, or name, or even memory –
And because we're all dead without You, all grey,
Even as alive as we seem to be

                       we sing, we sing slowly

Bless the Lord, my soul
And bless His Holy Name
Bless the Lord, my soul
He rescues me from death

And as we sing, all of my death rises in me,
All of my grief, fringed with silver like tears.
I see I'm nothing without You – but with You
As you move into my heart and among us like rain;
Rain falling, grey falling, where no rain is but feeling,
Grey falling, rain falling on a graveyard at the end,
And I'm standing in the rain in You, and I am alive!
Alive like the rain and the tears in your eyes
As we bless, blessing the soul we're made of,
Luminous like the rain, our eyes closed to the rain,
The song on our lips where we are dying into You,
Our love, our dying – dying into Love

Bless the Lord ...

And the silence takes us
While we sit before you open the door into the light ...

I leave the closing café with you Val;
I walk with you, and I walk alone
Even as we talk – with all this on my mind –
The day, its journey, and what I have to bring:
What can I bring down if I have no joy to bring?
What have I still got to shed, to leave behind,
That no one can do for me, no touch, no reassuring smile?

I take you up to show you the Well you've never seen.
The wind blows in our hair; we're still separate
After all we've shared, because I am in myself
Even when you reach briefly for my hand;
I'm plunged into something out of reach of speech
As we sit by the Well and close our eyes, waiting,
And the Well is deeper than I have drunk ...
Until out of the depth of it, out
Of the heart of the spiral
                    Your face comes

Your face in the depth, meeting mine. You and I.
The whole thing between us – in all of us –
                              is You and I.

Face to face where no sunlight is,
Face to face where there is no sound or solace,
You come, where there is nothing left but You –
You come out of the depth of souls and bodies
And you say again silently *I am in you.*
And the tan water shifts in the breeze ...

Then as we stand, the sun!

The sun's path over from the west, gleaming gold,
Molten gold, hammered on the water in light ...

> as I breathe

Thank you as I go out of myself, seeing,
And inside as the light in me rises to meet it ...
Both, and even as you say,
'It's a path, but I don't know if it's mine,'
Out of the blue, out of the future, comes gold again
Taking us there if we can let it.

As we turn and look down over the Strath
To the northwest shoreline, and the sea there,
First of all the rocks, then the waves around them,
Whitening as they crest and swell becoming something, *look!*

You point to it, blackening, gleaming over the sea's blue
Clear above the water for a moment – *'It's the whale!'*
And yes, you say softly as we stare out together
To where its tail rises briefly as it sinks

> becoming a line of moving black rippling

> *I am here*

As large as that, leviathan, and out of our hands,
Haunting us with the hope that its body keeps spelling,
Saying it without anything but *whale* and sunken water

> *in your speechless wonder*

Saving us:
To look, see, feel, think again
As your eyes remember, and you bow your head.

Down we go to our service now,
Hurrying to get there by the bell, as the light
Goldens over the evening grass, slanting in by the open door,
Its particles lit up like a swathe, as we enter,
Cloaking the building in the one light of the day
Come to rest, from the sky:

We sing the old pilgrim hymn, John Bunyan's,
That spelt my chosen path from the beginning,
Just as I sang it then, far above the assembly hall
And its rafters, into the green of shimmering trees
Where the summer morning light was, and I was walking
Free of hurt and loneliness, in a parallel time –
Another, nearer time where the building broke away
And I was on the road I'd always been on:

Then fancies fly away!
He'll fear not what men say,
He'll labour night and day
To be a pilgrim.

And I think of your Green Book where it all began,
With its gold-edged pages 'in the similitude of a dream'

As I walked through the wilderness of this world

Where it's always been this journey …
And now you pray in the tongues of different faiths;
The glossolalia of speech covers the air like a skein
Where we're all talking at once, from church to temple,
Synagogue to minaret and tabernacle, mountain;

Now all the air falls silent –
To the one light coming down over our heads
That has no name or form or liturgy, only presence

The Presence that is You
                 in all Your disguises

As we sit, and the silence of the walls is singing,
Singing with a light that is silent inner light,
Light within light, reaching each of us as it is,
In the moment that it is, flaking down like snow,
Dust-gold-light
                    telling us what we each need to know

In the name of worship, that is sacred attention ...

            – your breathing beside me
                    your energy as fresh as dew –

As we stand and say the Peace Prayer,
Beloved of All Nations:

LEAD ME FROM DEATH TO LIFE, FROM FALSEHOOD TO
    TRUTH.
LEAD ME FROM DESPAIR TO HOPE, FROM FEAR TO TRUST.
LEAD ME FROM HATE TO LOVE, FROM WAR TO PEACE.
LET PEACE FILL OUR HEART, OUR WORLD, OUR UNIVERSE ...

As the light
                becomes it

And as

I danced in the morning
When the world was begun

We dance, You dance as you are the dance,
We dance standing still as You weave among us
And You dance beyond all we know but the dance
That is Shiva and Shakti, Krishna and Tara,

That is all the names of compassion You arise in,
That is the colour in all skies and cities,
Flowers of the Lebanon and the dust of every desert rain,
Grail-bearer, chalice-bearer, sword and cup,
Blood and Beloved in all seasons and places,
White silence and awe in every lover's eyes

Christ of the heart and the innermost sky

As we chorus

DANCE THEN, WHEREVER YOU MAY BE,
I AM THE LORD OF THE DANCE, SAID HE,
AND I'LL LEAD YOU ALL, WHEREVER YOU MAY BE,
AND I'LL LEAD YOU ALL IN THE DANCE, SAID HE.

And still in the silence there's something deeper
That is the Father of Sound behind all sound,
The Father of Sound and the Mother of Breath, as you begin
The O that becomes the M –
As we sing it, sung then
We are the Song sung
OM

We are the note sung
From the depth and the height
and the depth that is the height

Drawing in around us, around our heads ...
Till there is nowhere to look but the centre,
No where to breathe but to the centre,
Nothing to believe in but the centre

where we are One Breath –

One Breath of the sea, and the whale rising,
One Breath of the sky and the Song beyond song

One Breath centring us
Were we leave all our creeds and skins behind and enter

One Breath
           beyond breath
                    that is the belly of dawn

Even as a handful of you leave, uncomfortably,
It goes into the silence till there's only our presence
Bowed in silence, and I stand to speak the blessing ...

Peace, deep peace where there's no church or temple
But only the living air around our heads –
Peace, deep peace where the running wave you see
Is the real wave breaking on to the shore –
Peace, deep peace where the quiet earth is silence
Humbled to all we don't yet know –
And the shining stars fill the dark above our heads
Where the roof has broken open into wonder.

We walk in the dark now, talking about love,
Not the love we've known, but the new beginning –
And is it new or ageless? It is seeing
That the love we have is given, and is over our heads,
Out of our hands, yes! Seeing us – seeing down
In the round circle of its dance we begin to enter
When we see its threads woven among us
And how we're each drawn together, into each other,
To stand in each other, and so we are company
Holding each other in this luminous space inside
In the one heart we're in, boundless as the sky.

I tell you about Shiva and Shakti – carved
From a single elm block base, seated together
Where all their light and dark rises in the grain
Into the bowl they're offering above their heads –
Offering all they are at the edges of their eyes, letting go
As you made them, George Ineson, with God in your eyes ...

And as we walk we talk out all the difficulties
Of emotion and reaction, jealousy and possession,
All the fear that blocks the sky from entering,
Grinding us inside, emptying us to receive it
If we choose it, if we can dare to let it be –
If we can dare to let the old skins burst as they are breaking,
Love and rage running all over the place! Nigredo,
Wine and grief in the gutter, running red and drunken
Until the cool wind of the spirit blows and we know
That wherever we are we can be in Love
And that Love can guide us to what is right.

But I don't know; how can I? And you? You say
All you knew was the joy of letting go,
Letting go of yourself when you first arrived,
Thinking, *'I'm somebody – and who are all these people?'*
And *'What am I doing living on a bunk in a broom cupboard?'*

You were joyous then, and I wanted you
 – to be in a dark place with you, to feel it –
As we walked towards the beach in the dark
And all I could do was let go of my mind – gone
As the stars are gone; I face you in the dark

Blind as I offer you my eyes
And we stand there holding each other,
Your face half Indian in the lightless twilight,
In the light where there is *no* light ...

And in the giving back and forth between us, surrender,
All surrender, and honouring, as you say,
'Peace be with you, brother'

                      and I feel it

Reaching from your arms down into your feet
And with your gift as it walks inside me. *Peace.*

Day 22

Iona

I dream the fronds of a spider plant
I'd cut back (because of moving)
                              to its roots —

And now there's no one to look after it;
It's been a terrible mistake. Ashamed, I realise
That even if I bury them, it's still going to die.
The only hope there is
                    a vivid patch of grass at its centre.

Meaning?

Four fingers of window-light
On the carpeted floor in front of the altar cross,
Four fingers of glimmering light
                              like the fronds

And the phrase you quoted from Penn, Tom,
About the unbelievers, echoes in my mind:

Help us not to despise or oppose
What we do not understand
                    as I heard it.

We sing 'Enemy of Apathy'
Like an acid that burns us awake
And strips off our complacency lest we forget
This is an edge we're living on where we never fully know
Your Edge
          your razor's edge
                        awakening

– a line of silver almost too sharp to see –

As you echo it, reading:

Instead they find joy in studying the Law of the Lord
*   and they study it by day and night.*
They are like trees that grow beside a stream
*   that bear fruit at the right time,*
*   whose leaves do not dry up.*
They succeed in everything they do ...

And you do! bringing your joy to me
And the light inside the building out with you ...
As I stand outside the door, leaning on the porch,
As you emerge, spreading your arms –
Holding me lightly and closely, before you turn to her:
'I don't know – I just want to hug everyone!'
As the light in you leaps
                  you turn the morning round,
It infuses me ...
All the shadows of my waking gone like lightning,
And I know
         it must be joy
               where everything opens

– the eye opens as wide and generously as the sky.

It's that I go to the mountain for now;
For *that* I'm climbing ...

The lane clear in the morning light,
The breeze clear in my lungs and legs as I stride,
The sunlit grass rising, as if effortlessly,
Knowing each twist of tussock and rock, knowing the way now,
And with the strength of ten, with a strength beyond muscle,
Not even having to pause to catch my breath

with the blue overarching blaze of the sky

Arriving alone, standing
As the light spreads everywhere:

JOY
       that is my name
               and yours, your song

Four fingers of light ... and the four
That is wholeness, circling, earth, completion

As the joy you spoke smiles on

And this light You sent that came
              in the angel of your face

Joy to let go to,
Light in your bare hands,
Sweetness of Creation in your mouth
To bring down

Joy that is the light
Deep peace, the healing
The whale has come to bring ...

Joy, and you shed your dead skin,
Joy, and you are born,
Joy, and you call into the wind

          the joy of every living thing
            of every being

To lull these faces as one, and then
             we are together in the light

In the light over everything

And we are one heart   with flower and stone
And we are one heart   with the cattle and the birds
And we are one heart   with the surfacing, plunging whale

As the whale says: *One,*
I am come from the Deep;
I have come in God's name
To show you healing and show you your hearts

And the Word is made Flesh in this light, in every living thing.
The scripture is wind, the words are stone and water,
And the Word is air that is ruffling over the waves,
And the Word is earth that the light's shining down on,
And the Word is the Dove to the outstretched man

The Words its wings hovering over him ...
The Word, the Dove penetrating through him

and that is yet to come, the eagle says:

First, strip away all the outer trappings.
First, cast aside all the skins of your name.
First stand naked, letting the wind cover you.
Stand in the light. Let the light flow through you.

John, I call you
    John, I come through
        John, until you
            see Love down

Until you see Love down
    every way like a star
        until you see Love down
            in every direction now –

And everywhere is the same

              one ray of your looking

To the left and the right and behind you

And as you turn you are a circle of the sun

As you stand in the cross you are the circle

As you stand you are the sun's rays, shining

And what the heart breaks in tears are the waters of your birth
       and the tears running down are the living water
           the water of healing, the flowing of tears
              not of blood, but of water now ...

Grace around you, grace above you,
Christ in the wind, Christ calling you

Be my son, be joyous, my son
Be still, be at peace, my son

Step by steps through the days of your turning
As you turn, and turn, and turn again:

I am the sound of the running streams and laughter,
I am in the gentleness of each small flower,
And what I am in you is *all* of you:

Christ to the North,
To the South and to the East,
Christ to the West.

Now lie down in the wind and breathe out, out, out ...

Come, Holy Spirit
Breathe in my name
Come Holy Spirit
Open my heart

Come Holy Spirit
Flow in my blood
Come Holy Spirit
That I come down

And the song says

Oh come and be born in me, Lord of my heart
Oh come and be born in me, Lord of my name
Oh come and be born in me, Lord of the wind
Oh come and born in me, Lord of the ways …

But I'm half born. Something is missing.

If I could say it like this, play it like this
As the piano stretches under my fingers
In the empty community room while you go off outside;
If I could say it with these two hands, to the left and right
The way one plays high and the other finds the bass notes
And the high approaches the low that shadows it
As it has to, as the black notes wait and well;
Gaining strength as the high notes stumble, then sadden,
As the high voice cracks without its companion
That is soul in the dark and the depth of the shell,
Depth of this body where the oyster yields the pearl
In the grit ground down like grief within it
So joy meets its other side, as man meets woman.

The slippery climb, the slippery mountain
– like you said, Mother Julian of Norwich –
Where we take three steps up to slide one back,

And what else for but what we've left behind?
How else is it but what we find we have to bring
So deeply into our being it's like swallowing,
Or else it can't *be body*, it can't be born for real.
I think so, Mother, and you knew it.

So what does it mean to go down to the *other* mountain,
To the mountain underneath, and wake there?
What does it mean as it I sit here waiting
To be hardly even able to see the view,
Only the mountain repeatedly inverted like a V
Reflected in blue water to its depth beneath?
Whale-black mountain
                              blue water
                                          blue air

And how do I get there?

There must be a third place where they meet.
And I see it. It is the circle, the circle of stones
                                                      the Cell

I must find it.

And I can't find it!

I go back over the terrain, tracing the way we came,
Down in the heather grass and boggy ground
Among the outcrops where everything looks the same
And everywhere are beginnings of circles among the stones,
But none of them is the place.

I wander absurd in the heat, yearning like a madman
For the point of balance, and missing it

And it's like this: I'm given to wander without a skin,
To know how much I need it.

I circle and circle until I'm lost
In the wilderness of waste and dreaming, this desert,
No circle ... no eagle ... no guidance, even ...

And the Dream is where the dream becomes the real thing,
Life or death – living it ...

I don't give up – but I have to let go.
It's not my timing.

Finally, I come round to the centre
And find you quietly gardening, Ralph,
With your blond hair, azure eyes, and Columban beard.
As you lean on a fork, the light on your face,
You look as if you've always been here.
We stand together and talk and you tell me
How notoriously difficult the place is to find:
'Everyone seems to get lost looking for it' – as you smile
With the light in your eyes and voice that is the message.

When I ask you about your journey you tell me
About the breakthrough you made when you were a pagan
So you *knew* ... and even as you're telling me I know,
Or it's as if I do, as the light moves between us,
Out of the silence of your eyes behind what you're saying
As you meet mine, without needing to look away,
So I can see Him in your face, Him in your body
When you say, 'I was high for a year. I was just living it.'
You let go of who you'd been, writing, everything
But your moment-by-moment being as it entered in

As the bridge ends here, and it ends between our feet,
Brother, though I barely know you;

We can't be strangers to one another in this light
That's the same between us and so simple it needs no drama
As I leave you turning back to it, with a wave –

and go to find *you*.

As we come back straight from supper in the sultry air
The guide appears – Pete, who happens to be passing.
He draws us a map in the air with his finger
Along the Ridge: *left, left, left.*

We walk the Ridge of the Way, along its green back,
Falling in step while it runs straight before petering out,
Skirting the bog, thick with kingcups and myrtle,
Testing the ground at its edge …
Then under a wire fence I hold up for you,
And over a second, holding it down, and the ground opens
Round an outcrop of rock, in the middle of nowhere again
 – '*But this must be right!*'

And as we go through the thighs of the Querns
'*There it is!*' breathing relief –
Down there on the glowing grass

the glowing green-gold grass, in the evening light.

We go down to it
And – 'You first' –

                          decide to take it in turns.

You go in and sit while the midges gather.
I give you my coat to cover your head like a cloak;
You pull it over and around you
                          as I climb back

Leaving you space for the gold of your moment.

The midges gather, and the sea is hushed.
It is so still. As the ground pulls down
And you sit with a coat for walls and a roof
You go invisible; you could be anyone ...
Woman, feeling the ground of your being;
Woman, feeling it rise in your body.

You stand up, suddenly yourself again:
'It's all yours – I'm getting bitten to death!'
As you climb back up in the breeze and the silence.

What do these stones give? There's an entrance.
What does this ground give? I must pause here.
I trace the saving sign over my chest
And I don't care about the midges for this moment –
It's too late for anything less.

Go to the centre now and stand.
Spread your arms in the four directions. And I do.
Now come into the centre and sit down.
Be quiet and give yourself over to the ground.

Quiet as the sea is quiet and as the air is still,
Let me forget myself and listen. Listen well.

And then who's here? Only I am,
Feeling the ground soaking under my thighs ...
But something missing – You.
Someone is missing. It has to be You.

I move back from the centre, inviting You in
To sit cross-legged on the ground, facing me.
Then you come in as simply, palpably,
As the gold around your tanned skin
Because you asked me.

How can I reach you? *Your heart.*
You say it without even lifting your hand.
I am your heart, within you, reaching it.
And that's all in the world I have to do
To be here ... in your dissolving.

What do you leave me? The ground
Where I lie outstretched, face down,
Pulling my coat up over my head
As you speak from the ground within,
From inside the darkness and the grass on my skin
As you say

I am sky
And I am earth
I am fruit
And I am ground
All things come together
In My Name.

Height and depth are one, and the mountain is one,
Is the only place there is that's the centre –
And in you as you stand there, beloved sensual man,
Putting the almond blossoms to your face, as Gibran saw you,
As my heart breathes into you, down into the ground.

Roll now, roll, roll over,
Roll over like a dog, roll it into your skin,
Silently exulting and laughing ...
And then I'm ready to move on.

You come down from your rock-perch towards me,
And as you hold my hands open resting in your palms
The sun is gold on the water – new, yellow gold –
And the Hollow and the hollow in my heart are filled with light.
And I thank you.

As we start back, there's wildfire between us,
Wildfire leaping across the divide – you know it,
Contained as we walk, and then you sing
Like a woman who knows her whole body is singing;
You half-hum the notes
                            and the bell is greeting us

The bell, and the voices of the kids playing cricket,
And Bluebell the horse, white, untethered as she sidles.
All these moments, ours, as the breeze is the wind's ...

We go in separately,
Each of us *'to be with God on our own'* as you put it
As we arrive for the Act of Commitment: to make it
As naturally as the rain, or the waves in the sea.

And it's for each of us, deep within.
I glance at you sitting alone, your face in its glow;
Then you close your eyes and go there, and I do the same.

In the beginning, God made the world

MADE IN LOVE FOR MAN AND WOMAN

And the women say

Womb dark and lifeless, You knitted us with love

And the men say

Growing and grappling, You grasped us with love

Wandering and doubtful, You held us with love

SUFFERING AND SICKENED, YOU HEALED US WITH LOVE

And you lead us all into You,
Deeper and deeper into each circle of love
As the words we speak warm the air like fire
With a strange sure warmth around my heart:
Call it fire, or call it Desire – *it is Yours*;
It's where the tongue of true worship begins.

And you know it as you say it, Muriel,

Come, come wherever you are
Wanderer, fire-worshipper, lover of leaving
Come – ours is not a caravan of despair

Even if you have broken your promise a thousand times
Come, come again, come

– Jalaluddin Rumi, your words burn in my mind:
An awe that begins in my throat, amazed
As you bow your head, letting them hang in the air
As they sear across the silence, as I want them to.

Don't you want to undress to the Beloved?
Don't you want to dare the full nerve of your heart?
Don't you want your fears to die like lightning?
Then come.

And I pray to be that broken, open-hearted

as we sing

Will you come and follow me
If I but call your name?
Will you go where you don't know
And never be the same?

We stand one by one, to come forward
To the altar edge where we wait in a line

And it's as simple as waiting, kneeling, and receiving
As you whisper a phrase alive in our ears,
Touching us each gently on the head.

'If you are thirsty, come to me and drink'

So I drink
                    and the air is wine,
The water is wine, and there's no regretting
Anything that hasn't been outside love.
All of it comes back now as You come

And the rest is sitting stunned as I wait for you,
Is red erasure streaking across the chairs and pews
Because there's nothing real outside of love
And love is all that moves in my blood and yours,
And when you take away the rest, or it's taken

You have the God of Love in your hands.
                                        Come.

Day 23

Iona

The blaze of fire
                    and what burns through in us

— and what it burns for love, in love

'in your eyes', no, in every cell!

Where the symphony of your body is ablaze
                                        it is invisible

And now

Brother man and sister woman, born of dust and passion
Praise the one who calls us friends, and makes us in like fashion

— so you say it

And the fire is earth, is clay, is compassion,
Is our natural selves calling on us to return
To what we were made from in You —
                                    Eve, Adam

Made like that, made in passion
Not calculated, modelled, and freeze-dried for God's sake!
Not made to be bound, obedient, and tame
                                    but tyger-eyed

        where the lion lies down with the Lamb —

And now

O God the spirit
You in love move us
Who once was nowhere
And felt unknown,
We give our need of
You for our companion;
All things can change
When not on our own

– so we pray,
The inner voice attuned and listening,
Attuned into You as you move without ending,
Evolving from inside the flowering white belly of your Being
Where the petals infold, sheathed, against the night sky ...

Now outside, as I stand facing the sea
The rising edge of the cloud is like a shark's mouth, over Mull,
Where the hole of the sun is an eye ...
And the wind blows one world across from the shore
Over the slate-grey water of the Sound like a lake

As I take the card I'm posting you –
Arranging to meet you back here to walk.

It doesn't happen. Or not like that.
When something else is being planned in our plans.
I come back, but you don't seem to be around –
Or maybe I go the time wrong. Anyway I have half an hour

And come back to the Nunnery; wouldn't be here otherwise.

I round St Ronan's Church with its red walls
As the sun comes out from behind a cloud,
Gleaming on the grass its shell is broken open to;
I wander along the edge of the wall footings and enter

Into the cloister, with its invisible flame windows,
That's become a garden, reclaimed.

And the Spirit hangs in the air;
The spirit of the women moves among the flowers,
So present you half expect to see them
(These invisible companions to their brothers).
The Father has an Abbey; the Mother has a Garden
Where the sea swings and you can be with the summer ground.
She has everything she needs ...

I wander in the cloister to the edge of the wall
Where it opens into the enclosure of the church.
Is it the sun in my eyes? Is it the quiet air
Gathering into the calm that was yours
So I can feel you inside it as if you were here?
How is it that as I lean into the opening arch
I know you were here, and are?

I go in and sit by the single bay chancel,
Sliding slowly down, my back against the wall
Where the light slants on to my face
And you are here in the light brightening through the flowers
Vivid in their colours in the grass; I lean back
And they meet at the horizon of my eyes –
The close horizon that is their being in front of me
As if flowing out of themselves, from within,
All one as I'm seeing them – so clearly –
As I see you in them, and you are in the whole of them,
You are their breath and being, and you could be
Outlined at their edges and at all the light's edges

As you say *feel this with your heart, this lightness,*
And see this is the Mother, and I am in Her.
All you see of me now is Her, where I belong ... as I gaze

And all you say is light bathing, breaking over me like a wave,
Mother, in the light you were and are and you died into.

Mother, and you'd said you'd be here. I'd forgotten.
Mother, guide and friend, where the light is unending
As you cross each threshold in your innermost being
Inwards to the radiant core we are
Mother
               and the sun gently slips away
Even as the light stays behind my eyes and fades
Leaving your gift, which I breathe in
With the hyacinths, the grass, and the Michaelmas daisies,
The irises, dahlias, and clover and the miniature roses
And the whole light soul of the ground, which is my own now …

As I walk away, seeing it's time,
The slit window gleams over the rubbled earthen floor
And the sun is white
               high in the dove-mist

Above Maclean's Cross
At the turning –

       and the light will follow you
            in all the shades that are its own.

I come back to the crowded room
Where you're talking about the week and what it's been
And what it means to cope with differences, and the pain
Of being different (as if we could be anything less)
As your human faces fill the space, with you
Pouring your twenty-eight-year story out …

Yours too, when you talk of the barriers coming down,
With your tanned face, and I see you there in the glory,
Cutting people's hair in the heart of the city …

And what does it mean to take Iona with us?
We all have a different work to do, but don't be fooled,
All that matters is that we do it with love –
And then we're *all* of what we do, more than its sum.
None of us could be placed, the way we are here,
Drawn out of our lives into the light of our being
Like boats in a bay, someone said, *floating in harbour* ...

Then what do our differences mean? We have to go
Beyond all -isms and even religion, to see
Where all our colours are transcended in the rainbow
Arcing over the grey and its rain, overlighting us.
That is our Covenant, and to see it with Your eyes too,
To accept each other where we are, and precisely
In the mystery of what we are, which is the work You do.

When we've crowded into lunch, your moment comes –
Long after the grace and the announcements.
You stand up, as if you've suddenly decided, to sing
'Dear little buttercup ...' You preface it saying,
'It should really be sung by a little thing with a lisp.'
In the swing of it you're past caring: it's innocence;
It's a naked old man become a child againm
Your voice cracking as you raise your half-closed eyes:

Dear little buttercup
Dear little buttercup
Dear little buttercup – I

And outside, softly falling, the rain begins.

'Shall we go for that walk then?' I meet you, Liz,
With your blond face and eyes the colour of the day.
You go to fetch your anorak and boots, and Dorothy,
And we set off in the rain

                              in this cloak of rain

267

Coming down from the grey-white sky round our shoulders,
A brooding breast, as we gaze up at the change.

The land goes matt in its dun, furrowed harvesting
In the fields behind us. We branch down the Machair lane,
Where a streak of yellow wet paint blurs to the edge
In an arc across the tarmac where the light is dissolving;
The sky stretching overhead down to the bay
Along the single cable-line, to where the lane peters out
To the grass opening towards the sea.

As we walk you talk about returning here to faith
With the change that being under this Island sky brings;
This *'sky of vision'* we call it, seen like a poem
Where the lines are centred vertical, reaching us like waves ...
The rain thickening, we reach the sand's edge
And the bay opens out like embracing arms

                                              where we sit

The rain dripping down your hoods, gleaming on your faces
In the sheen of the air ...

                              before you decide to move,
Leaving me here, back into the mist that takes you
As I surface alone to walk on the sand.

Suddenly, it could be ten years later
And this dream I've woken from
To find that it's raining and you've all gone.

Ten years later. Or twenty-eight ... Who knows?

I walk, gazing down – large shingle in the stones
Thrown back and back by strong waves and storm,
But it's all calm, now, where the rain pocks the sand ...
The bay at the back of the Island spreads like a bow
And the rain's a cloak of space come down to walk away in:

The sunlight gone behind us like a dream
Stained into glass in Eternal Summer Light,
The earth comes in, the rain shrouding it in quiet,
And now we have to take it inside, all of it,
Living it here where it belongs, as far as we have come.
 I think of you here, Gwyn, as you drift back saying,
'The pilgrimage has no ending.' It's all of our lives.
The breadth you named becomes the Bay

Where the gulls wait on the shore as the waves ebb in,
The rocks spread on either side, where two oystercatchers sit,
Two fisherman in oilskins go on working, as it streams down,
And the whale vanishes out to sea under the mist ...

And as I walk I can't remember what's behind me,
Nor can I see ahead. It's all unknown –
There's only this breadth of You, and the whole-hearted giving,
Where the river reaches the sea and swells, fanning into the ocean.

The rain soaks my head and the backs of my legs;
The whole earth comes wet and gleaming here – like a birth –
And we say *take your journey to the end and it ends in bliss,*
It ends in One Being – and it ends in our solitude
As we scatter slowly out across the plain ...

   one by one, we walk on the sand
            one by one, we walk in the rain like images
      one by one, in each pause of our thinking
               as we come back to the mystery of what we cannot know.

These steps in the sand the waves will wash away;
These sand-steps the waves will wash clean.

As the prophecy reads:
Iona shall be what it was.
I come back soaked like a laundry, to change,

The rain still fresh on my hair and face.
I tell you it's like my eyes have been cleansed, too,
As we meet outside: where shall we go? The shrine.

We round the cloister wall where St John's Cross
Stands like a guardian against the thin keyhole door.
We open it over the threshold into the dim light
Where an altar flame glows red day and night.
And as we sit we sink, deep into the quiet
Like a solid block of gold air reaching down,
Deep musk gold, like an incense
In the concentrated depth of your body

And there's nothing to do but be still and pray
Till suddenly in the warmth that steals into my chest
I'm seeing you one by one … and as it builds
I see each of your faces in the Rose
As we turn to face each other, like a dance
But a dance that's deep red stillness
Where we see each other as we are in our hearts:
Carole, Jehanne, Gabriel; Rob, Steve, and Will.
It's only as we interweave to make the Rose
In the company we secretly are that I ask
That we all find love and strength, now;
May we each come to live in one another's hearts.

We stand for a moment in the porch, and you ask me
How it will be when you're back there with him –
And nothing is simpler, or could be,
Than the phrase that comes straight out of my mouth
As it did from yours long ago, and is ours now, out of time:
'I will be in you' – and you smile, knowing.

'There speaks John,' you say, his cross between us
Shadowing the rain-light in your shining eyes.
Then it pours, torrential.

And as we go into Communion
The violin is playing its own song, its love song
Weaving lightness through the candlelit air,
Gold thread to a bird's beak, lingering ...
We sit together as it flies free around us –
Not freed of sadness, but free to feel all it feels,
Call it all the threads that move between us,
Moving in love, needing each other to be what they are,
Seeing it's all one in the pulse of your hand;
And as making love is life and art, food and breath,
Amen to the God of Life, we say *Ameyn*, we promise.
I hold the Rumi poem you've written out by hand,
And all the warmth in the world could be in us now
And under these eaves, pulsing like a transmitter.

We stand: you say

*When the lights are on and the house is full, and the laughter is easy, and all
    is well*

Behold, I stand at the door and knock

*When the lights are low and the house is still, and the talk is intense, and the
    air is full of wondering*

Behold, I stand at the door and knock
                                    and You do

And we are the house, in our skins,
As you knock to the rhythm of our hearts
Where the door is, where You're trying to come in –

*And tonight, always tonight, as if there were no other people, no other house,
    no other door*

Behold ...
>   there is no other door, no other way

And when we ask you in, stranger,
We can say

FOR THE DOORS OF THE HOUSE WE OPEN, AND THE DOORS
  OF OUR HEARTS WE LEAVE AJAR

For we sing what only the song knows,
Sung within itself, behind the words,
In its slow processional of gladness
To the open heart of its lilting refrain:

THEN SHOW YOUR FACE AND TAKE YOUR PLACE
AND SHARE YOUR TIME AND TREASURE
WHERE NO ONE LESS THAN CHRIST THE KING
TAKES REFUGE AND BRINGS PLEASURE

And your pleasure is this,
That a child should read the Gospel,
Scanning quickly over the words, as unashamedly
As if he were relaying a message to a friend –
Isn't that how You meant it to be sent?

We stand now, and it's *their* turn,
All the little ones in the world, dressed up
In party gear with glitter and masks, moving towards the table,
The long table in the centre with the cloth for supper;
They giggle and shuffle, in and out of line,
And not even Fellini could have dreamt this ...

We sing a prophecy we know behind them

Since the world was young
There's a song that we've sung
Of a promise coming true

Hungry folk will eat
And lost-lost friends will meet
And the Lord will make all things new

You crash the tambourine: we raise the roof

GOD HAS A TABLE
WHERE HE CALLS HIS FRIENDS
TO A FEAST THAT NEVER ENDS

GOD HAS A TABLE –
AND ONE DAY WE'LL MEET HIM THERE …

And the violin takes up the tune,
Weaving its aftermath in with the flute
Till it's all quiet, the table is ready,
And you begin to invite us to the sacrament …

You tell us the story we know, transformed
In the light of our gathering where it's all of us,
And as we closen into something we've never seen
We cross the divide and the waters are broken.

Come. It is the Lord of the Morning who invites you in

As we eat and the bread and pass the cup, we know it:
Morning has broken like the rain in the dawn.
As we sit in the darkness that is the dawn rising
And our faces in this light are its testimony
Our Communion is ours with all of you
Scattered everywhere out of the locked churches
In the cities of dread and the dark country lanes

Where you walk watching the lights burn in the valley,
Wondering if there is even a piece of sky left ...

And as you lead us back
                              the sky bursts with light
                  as it bursts with rain —

        and we sing, past caring

        when all that matters is the joy of the Song

WE ARE MARCHING IN THE LIGHT OF GOD
WE ARE MARCHING IN THE LIGHT OF GOD

Marching with you, Mother Africa,
Marching with all the slaves there are,
Polluted, compromised, disenfranchised —

Tribes of the Bushmen, tribes of Australia,
Tribes of the Plains, the Andes, and the Silence,
Tribes of the Lord with our faces in gold,
Tribes of all our faces, like the dream,
Tribes of all our skin, become One People
Marching

WE ARE MARCHING

The roar of the Song rises like fire
Into the arches of the roof, become light
As the door lies open and you lead us out
With the tambourine bashing, in and out of time,
And we are

MARCHING IN THE LIGHT OF GOD

On a tiny Scottish island –
But I hear the roar sweeping over Europe
Into Rumania and the ghosts of Tiananmen Square,
Into the heart of old Yugoslavia …
A roar that no one can contain or withhold
As eerie as the wind sweeping through the trees,
Flung against the light as the candle stays burning
And the wind only makes it larger and brighter.

What is the Miracle of Light that can bring us
Out of the catastrophe of our falling?
How else can we reach the Kingdom but here?
Show us Your face, Lord, show us Your fire
So we can know it as our own as we march to the dawn.

Show us Your face, as we bring it down softly
And I wake among the refectory tables
Where you're singing the chant into your feet
And into the hush beyond our understanding.

You beckon me, questioning me with your eyes. We slip away
To walk our last night while there's still time.
The darkness and the rain-air greet our faces
Now it's finally stopped: a few stars out – you glance up –
Beyond the shifting mass of invisible cloud …
Where are we going now? We're going to the end,
Where the lane takes us north to where we began.

Only, it's dark now when we leave the lights behind.
All I can see is the silver sheen of your earrings
That glimmer like discs in your soft, quick stride.
I'm losing your outline, and you've lost mine,
And there's only your hand in the dark, and your thighs
Moving through the black liquid air charged with static.
We're two black figures looking for a place

Two beings blending with the air that have no names.
You wonder if it'll rain more – and as I hear your voice
Your body breathes in a different, stronger silence
And it's as though we have to talk to remember we exist;
Strange, this, and not what we were thinking.
What is the secret of the darkness? It's beneath,
Snaking like a river through its own air and ground

Until we find where we're standing near the edge of the sand.
Dark sea and sky, dark grey. Dim shape of the mound –
All changed now, same place but so different
And no one else here, or near, as if they never were ...
But standing and keening your eyes till they hurt
You can see a silhouette like a ship,
A tall-masted ship in the bay – *and is it even there?*

Cool wind. We sit back against the dune;
You nestle a hollow as you shift and reach for me
And I can't tell where you end and I begin, only this.
Even when your hand falls gently back, the dark is good.
Cool wind, and we're alone now – human and abandoned –
Even though its presence shivers like a tingling ...

The rest would be an eclipse. So we leave it.
It's peace instead, then the wind turns cold. We start walking.
We start back, and the rain begins as it deepens –
Until it's so dark you can barely reach the gates,
Even your hand in front of your face, and there's nothing
But blackness everywhere, and the rain, blinding.
We lose our outline, then we lose our eyes.

How like them we are: we've left Paradise,
Expelled into primordial darkness, out of Eden.
And as we stumble I dream we walk down the centuries,
Holding each other's hand, trying to find our way
With only our feet to guide us; the Island submerged,

As if the landscape has lost all shape and definition ...
Fionnphort under water, only its neon lights showing.

Then a single roving beam out of nowhere
Spreading its arc of ghostly silent white
Searching out the sea and shoreline, for survivors.
Is this the end? Or have we reached it?
The plain of Armageddon stretches beyond our eyes,
Confusing sea and sky in a seamless black apocalypse
Until we glimpse the lights of the Abbey. With relief
We quicken our steps and breathe, and the spell is broken.

We sit in the shrine and touch – forehead to forehead
And all things are one in the dark: You in everything,
All in the heart now; the rest is scenery, a stage set.
Not even these ancient stones can do it for you ...

And in the Abbey a voice says *don't go in there now*,
The monks are praying in the dark, and it's their time.

Day 24

Leaving

S unlight fills the room,
 Sunlight pouring through the Chapter House windows

              all the way round

       and into all our eyes as I see them –

And as I ask, I receive: *Offer up your hands. Give thanks.*
Just so You know I received the gift
                     and I have.

There's no holding it,
No holding you
          or the river
                back.

There's no delaying either – we've got to pack up and go.
I'm pulling at the table, then the chairs,
Stripping the mattress and heaving it against the wall.
Leaving the sunlight pouring through into an empty room.
No trace, it was a dream; there was no one here at all.

We go into the service, arranging to meet,
For all the time there is, by the south exit door …
Sunlight fills the Abbey: I catch my breath as it shines
Through the king window behind the altar – and it's You
Without a face or form in the silence, only light
                         You

Glimmering in the flame-form of its shape.

We sing it now, we sing it all

For the beauty of the earth
For the beauty of the skies
For the love which for our birth
Over and around us lies ...

                     and as I catch your eyes

Christ our God to thee we raise
This our sacrifice of praise

  – and it's calm, calm as the day
As we toast each other with cups.

The window glass gleams over us as the words go
(Although I say them all, and still)

THIS IS THE DAY GOD HAS MADE
LET US REJOICE AND BE GLAD IN IT

This is the day He makes when he lets go ...

I stand for a moment, then move with the flow
Of you out towards the main door, then round on the grass
Where the sea opens out – to the presbytery door:

                            you're there

With five minutes before you go to work.
I don't know what to say, it's all so fast,
There's only your face and eyes, then I know
What else. It's *thank you*, in the given time
As I hold your hands, for your gift of prayer
And you say mine was passion – like the last things
We'd say before we reached the Light –
As the sun brightens beside you.
All that was true was this, too –

'We didn't waste a moment' – and you know as I do
That all that was truly true will remain

And the sun slants full on your face
Until there are only our eyes. Then you turn, and go.

I wander back to base, dazed with it all
As we gather there and the frame begins to unwind
And you talk about your time here, and all I can hear
Is *thank you*, as we thank you, Tom – and when I do
'I feel I'm just beginning to learn how to live ...'
Is all I can say, and from the bottom of my heart,
The light shining through on to our bowed heads and backs
As we let the silence briefly take us, then stand.

And it's all a song, only no one is singing,
No words or tune, only the sunlight –
And only pure feeling reaching down to the sea.

We come out to the cloister and I sit with you, Ann,
Yards away from the closed arch of your door
And we talk about priesthood and closed religious minds
Before we begin to walk, leaving the sculpture behind us
As you smile and gesture to its shape – *'That's it, you know'* –
And I do, and it's all of life in the leaving ...

We walk out on to the grass and round
Past the door down to the gate, and on to the leas.
The sun is blazing silver over the water
And we walk in its sheen, you glancing over into it.
I have come from the living to go with the dying;
In the deep light in your eyes and smile
There's only the light, so bright it could take you.
I lose your face and find it, then lose it again
Here on the edge of light – as you turn in mid-phrase,
Pausing as we walk and talk, and it's as if we know

That *the farthest shore is here* – without needing to say it –
Emblazoned in our minds with every step we're taking.

As we come down on to the jetty to board
You walk with us. It waits ... the sea swell, the ramp,
And your voice behind us calling,
'People keep coming, it's time!' as we walk on and turn.
'Come on, you've got to go – '
You all line up behind us as we crowd in the boat,
Throwing final words like scraps across the gap –
And then the distance slowly grows; you quieten, it all hangs,
You on your side, us here

                         then as the engines start

And we start to move, this is it now

                         you wave, you call,
You wave one by one, then all together

And as you wave, the gulls call; you wave, and the gulls wheel

                    metanoia, metanoia

As they cry and you wave, your arms raised
As the tears come ...
                    metanoia

As they wing, white wings, circling
Calling, singing, smiling, as you wave on
                         your hands fluttering
                         our hands
                         your hands

And we turn, we turn towards the Abbey,
We turn, we turn towards the mountain,
We turn towards the Sound and the open sea

As the Island begins to loom around its shore and recede –
The gulls reaching after us, still wheeling and calling

And all that matters in the Dream is your turning;
All that matters, even as it fades, is the turning
Because the turning is all that it's for

                              your returning

Turning, on this turning earth-sea

                    turning into God –

And I can't tell you how it's done

– only listen, listen, listen everywhere for the Song.

We nose back over the Sound's thin stretch
And in minutes the ground of Mull is under our feet again;
In no time at all, it takes no time –

We're boarding back on to the blue bus
That brought us all this way, parked up in silence.
In the quiet as we drive into the Empty Green Quarter
We're all facing forward with our eyes looking back
As if everything was the wrong way round – only sadness
Is what it means to have our hearts facing front
And nothing's wrong, you're only crying for what's natural,
And without tears, only a silence that can't speak
Because it's too close for words, and it's all of this;
You know as you gaze out *this is what being here is.*

Nothing but the green emptiness, lingering ...
Perfectly remote and unintrusive, a backdrop –
Until we pass two lochs buried deep in a mountain hollow,
Rising side by side as you break the silence, Margot,
Talking about religious narrow-mindedness, and that boy

'From Bigglesthwaite, was it?' and you chime in, Rosemary,
Telling us about your journey from South Africa ...
And mile by mile we come back to the ground,
Into the normality of divisiveness and doubting
Even as I see perfectly well what you mean.

Take care, we have just left the Dream
Take care, you are still waking up ...
Don't gag on the world too soon

I'm silent in my heart, thinking none of this
As the sky in front of us clouds to soft grey,
Not Emptiness now

                   but fullness, and retaining.

Don't let me lose a moment of this feeling

It is bearing the dream now

                   returning

As if the Island was a womb without walls behind us
And the silver blazing light an umbilicus –
Turned inside out as the silence forms a skin,
So that I'm outside and inside all I've been seeing

Still here, lingering

                   poised

In an in-between world that is both, simultaneously,
As we come into Craignure and wait for the ferry,
Eating dry bread sandwiches at the café ...
All of it passing, and it's still the Dream

And as I stand on the windswept deck in the open sea
It rolls back

              it all rolls back

Rolling towards me over the waves' crests and the foam,
Leaving the mountains inching back
                              the clouds piled low

Until the last glimmers of the line to it run back
Silver in the distance
                    over Ben More

And we turn into Oban Bay
                    and it's gone.

Who are we now? Our faces,
Bodies invisibly charged, changed beings,
We file off the ark, its looming black metal hull
Behind us. In the cark park, in the breezy light
We are our faces and, God, our faces are so open,
Yours warmed, yours tanned, your eyes shining
As we start this ritual of goodbyes ... so unreal
When it's now we should be saying *hello, I can see you!*
From smile to laughing smile as we circulate
And in the light of our faces where the sound cuts out
We're only the light of our meeting in this leaving
And there are no names or ages, anything;
We're seeds in a world that is only just beginning
And, different as we are, we're born to go far,
As far away and apart as we have come
                              and far on

The way the wind blows where it shall
                    the way

Nothing we can see in any of us guides us
                    this side, and beyond

In *Its* own time.

284

And do You blow in the litter round the streets
In the last wave and the vanishing lights?
Do You blow us like seeds where we're ready to float
And do You know which way we will land?

I don't know what this world-shadow intends,
Or if this Winter will become Spring again,
But I know this: *You are the pattern that connects,*
Illegible though the pages seem to be
Where they run past even our conceiving

Where You run out of sight of our minds.

                                        You've gone now.

Four pilgrims on the road south

                        the ramp goes down to London

And as we start the longest drive we draw inside,
Each to our own, suddenly, strangely alone.
You sit with your silver hair bunched, writing your journal,
A spiral notepad on your knee, as I write this ...
Pausing to lift our pens at the curves and bumps,
Glancing up, and you smile briefly and go on –
As the afternoon descends into silence and white road lines
Miles south to Glasgow

                        and south again

And I am like a dragon guarding a rich hoard
As its pieces start to glow like mosaic inside me,
Like jewelled light I'd give everything for
As I've been given it – and for the one place
Where they can only come together: in my upper chest
In the wide open whole of my heart ...

 – piano music, drifting out from the common room

— the Abbey walls, centuries blended in stone

And so You set me a task

and is that where the vow comes?

I made a promise, am making it now:
I will to create, to be with Creation
Heart soul and mind, skin blood bone, and spirit
To give of the gift You have given

Salvation.

I sing with the psalmist, with the Ancient of Days.
I sing with the flower too small to have a name.
I sing with those behind me, with those in front,
With those who sing through me and are unborn.
I sing as we circle, and as we sing we are companions
Singing in blood and in the deep riven strata.
I sing with the stone and the leaf, the rock and the stream,
And I sing with the angel hammering in the dark at your door.

I sing the song I'm given to sing
And it's not my song — it's ours for the taking:

Imagination, New Creation in the Dawn

And the Lord and the Mother of the Morning shall lead us

… as the colours blend, I fall asleep

dreaming the Island

Where the dreams we have dreamt are real

to-be-born.

I wake and take over the driving

into the grey light

While you map read
                    and the road skims by a hundred miles
As we try to make as much distance as we can.
Where else do we come to
                    too tired to go on

But Lockerbie? ... My mind loses focus;
It comes over me like rain. 'Tom, I think we should stop.'
You consult your watch and nod – nearly nine
As we cruise up and down the empty High Street
Trying for places, till finally The Bluebell –
We arrive in a hungry dream and back in chronos time.

Pilgrims? Anonymous now, as we began –
Four unlikely companions sitting together
Squeezed in at one table, each with a separate room ...
But inside the same as we wait to eat, gazing,
And I think of how we wear our badge like a secret,
As we said back then, Tom, in my little wooden studio,
Your face looming: 'This is who I always was.'

We talk on, about chaos
As our world speeds towards the edge
Of no return, our flawed humanity all over the news,
Weighed, out of balance, with the best out of sight;
And how else can the change come without this blackening?
How else can we make the leap,
This return of all returns unless we let go, seeing
That solution can only come like this, as messily as birth,
Or else we merely replace one structure with another
While the same power-hungry mendacity goes on ...?

And as the colours swirl like shadows in the Dream
As if exploding into liquid light behind my eyes, I see
That it is all one thing ... spreading like a flood ...
And we're the world inside being broken and remade

Even as we fight for the day.

This birth is all of us

— even when we lose sight of the bridge, and the landing.

We walk out for air, where the Island has gone,
On to the hard late street, veering left as we cross it
And following the sign to a Remembrance Garden
Down a quiet side pavement as the sky becomes the moon
Half full, reaching into the silence above the pines
As we talk about liturgy ... *and you come to me*
Across the distance like no distance. Its whiteness gleams
And brightens as I think of you, directly, into it —
Then my eyes fall back into the cool whispering breeze

Where I remember you now — *inside, everywhere* —
In the air we become ... as we stand silently, then turn
And the night is young, the Night is long ...

We wander back, Tom, talking about the real priests
Scattered everywhere among us — the laity
In our hearts now as we pause outside the door
And you tell me a story 'that Martin Buber tells,
About a boy who had a special rapport with a horse ...
He'd touch its mane, and always it would whinny and wait.
No one else could make it do that, no one could explain it —
But then one day he realised what he was doing
And he lost it, you know ... the magic went.'

'So having mastered one skill, you have to let it go again?'
'Yes, you have to return to the wilderness
But then you have to come to the marketplace again
Or the gift isn't used and it's wasted ...'
And you add, 'It's this constant tension between the two,'
As I meet your eyes, haunting the dark street with light
Like hollow blue fire — and thank you, as I do again now,

As I reach a hand on to your shoulder
Into the soul of all touching ...

I sprawl upstairs on the vacant double bed,
Sit up and stretch out my bare hot feet.
As the nightclub pounds its bassline from across the street
I think of how you could be here, and why you aren't,
And reach for a pen and these pages ...
And even as I think of the ease between us,
Of how you feel a part of me, and time is young between us,
I know that what's real here is your ghost, your innermost

And, yes, *the gift given as it is* – precisely like this
With a turning I have to make, south now to you
To face

Love in every direction, and nothing less.

Day 25

Returning

The dream is not behind us
It is in front of us —
It is the Dream that is dreaming us

Grey rain morning, a sheet of rain falling ...
Glimpsed through the white of the nylon half-curtains,
Over the hungover low of the party night street,
Over these restless, tangled, flung-back sheets
And oh, you know
     this is the Sad World waking.

The hiss of tyres passing, swishing in the wet
As I copy out your letter, and let it go.

Ash flakes down in the rain like snow
And there's nothing to do but wear the rain like a cloak,
No clothes but the rain, naked in feeling now.

Rain on my forehead
     rain, as it rained
          rain, as it began

— pour down, pour down,
Pour down your cleansing translucent song.

I am rich, and empty: full, and no one;
Enough to keep passing through with my hands free.
I step outside and back: 'How did you sleep?'
'Oh, I could have for a week ...' as you smile,
And we breakfast briefly before it's time to move on.

'OK, let's go' – the steel rails echoing
As I think of you, still up in Oban,
And you, reading the responses now –
And you in my heart of hearts, waiting.

I am full, and I am nothing. Blow through me;
Make me a reed to Your song –
Is this what it means to be reborn?

We drive out south into the rain and mist
                              like a bardo stretching into the sky

Where the road ahead blends with the wipers
                    and the border is unmarked where we slip over it –

Past the sign
Saying Cumbria.

                    So this is England …

        and the waters, like the rain, have broken

England gleaming like the Bay at the Back of the Ocean

With the sea teeming down from the sky

And this mist of the Machair you vanished in alone

And the road pushing us relentlessly on
                                        the ramp, the swell

And now the tide, hugely receding …

The arrow drawn
                    in the bow:

We come down into the peaks, landing
Among their green hill-hummocks as if from above
As the road curves down and round

                              under your roving wings

Before the long slow descent begins

And still the Land, Risen – I glimpse it from the wheel
In a V of deciduous trees on a steep upland slope …

I have been in the Summerland; it lifts
And quickens like a breath as the sky begins to clear,
Filling the sky inside my eyes again:

Buttercup – tormentil – white clover – harebell
Heather – bog asphodel – sundew – pimpernel

Garlanding the inner air as they weave
Their litany of names and colours, like a mantra
Shifting against the blue and becoming it,
Tinged with light, the light the blue rises into

– the whole Song made of substance and light –

Treasured light, cherished, detail by detail
That the light is infused in, to the smallest syllable:

And the sea was blue, Mediterranean blue and silver,
Silver against the gold of the sun it blended into
So that the light was silver, blazing like the moon.

The sky was blue, pale, cobalt, and azure,
And sunset-riven amber rose across its whole spectrum

And the living and the dead were alive together,
The dead at our roots, alive at our foundation –

At their time

        in their time

                and there was no time;

And you were dead, and yet alive in Her –
Alive in the Mother as you always will be
And part of the shadow of the silhouette at evening
And in the stillness of the light among the flowers

And I don't know *when* it is – but it's now,
You're telling me, Josephine, as the land quickens by –
Your silver hair, face, brown liquid eyes
Framed in the light you could be speaking to me from
Beyond time and yet here

                as the back seats judder.

You tell me, though you can put no name to it,
It's like a cloud you once saw around your head,
A cloud you knew was God as far as you could know anything,
And you knew then *'everything will be all right'*,
All things shall be well, all manner of things ...
And as I see you now, that cloud is around you
As everything goes still ... you lean back and smile,
The cloud of unknowing knowing around your face like a mist

      the cloud no rain or even sun can see by

Which wraps my head and touches me like breath
Hovering like an angel over the roof of the bus,
Hanging on by a feather – its body a whole streaming!

And suddenly everything is different, everything a skein
You penetrate beyond our wildest dreams
Faster than we can even symbolise – because it is
This air and everywhere screen, flashing by –
And it's air, blue paint, metal and tarmac, tyres

Transparent to the light as each particle of sun-dust
Hangs and moves like a wave
                              dancing, vibrating

And your cloud – this knowing, unknowing
The grief that matter is solid and unredeemable –
Stuck, pulped, ground to a halt, tangible.

                    But Life is always moving
                 – and that is the Dream

We pause briefly one last time, coming down,
At a little green café somewhere in Derbyshire
Hunched by a bend in the road – with
Its tables and chairs like a child's first house,
Where we lean over tea, the radio playing,
And the light streaming through wavering curtains
Breeze-blown from the draught through the door ...

And everything is open: the light on your face,
The stream rising from your cup ...
Everything is open though we say almost nothing.
Everything open, everywhere you can imagine:
The light in your eyes, the window veils, and the sky
                                        is glass

Then no glass, only structured space –
And the heart in freedom.

You take over driving, David, as we go now
With the light of the day open over our heads
For the main road to the main artery, and the End

 – into the heart of your home county,
Where the blue settles and the bus will vanish,
Leaving its box-wheeled shape for the sky ... while I stand

With the empty road, streaked in light, and the city in the haze.

When I sit back, the sky speaks above my head
In the inner sky it enters — as You guide me
In all your shapeless form and face
That is visible everywhere, unseen and attending
In the truth you are everywhere creating …

And all You say is Love; all you fill my mind with
Is think of what it means to say,
'I am only truly myself in Love.'

See what the letting go was — and be born
Your gift, and the gift of all of you is this
To be who you really are

And as the motorways join

                    the road speeds down

Heaven and earth accelerating —

And outside everywhere — harvest fields
The whole of the ground is gathering …

Bardo of rain

          and bardo of light

'My whole life was with me'

And as I say to you, somewhere in mid-sentence,
'If I trust my hands, my feet, and my breathing
They will take me to the deepest places of praise.'

                              Praise, Rilke,
Praise, you said
               'Praise, that's it!'
                         Praise, you knew it.

Praise, and the whole sky rises silently,
And the road, and your face driving, like a blessing.
Praise where the heart opens in light,
Releasing our eyes so we can see everything.
Praise in these last moments of our being
Because we are only always saying goodbye.
Praise, and it's only then we see

   strangely what was never lost

Our eyes seeing, but our eyes are blind
Until our hearts become our eyes.

So in the silence I'm thanking you one by one
For being exactly as you are, right here now,
And no more or less than I'd want you to be.
Before I say it
     we pull into the train station
And I go in to check the times, come back out
Haltingly as if half-disbelieving
As I meet your eyes ...

And as you wave I shoulder the burden that is mine.

The station platform bathed in light,
I'm sitting on a ledge with its window filled in,
Glancing down at the rails and the sunlight like gold
In a warm shaft like wind ... and how our darkness is unreal
If we could see it for what it is – *hiding*
For fear we'd have no freedom outside it.
        Is that right?

Fear is the evil, fear at the root of me,
Fear as I cling on, even to my baggage ... like ideology;
Then all I have is all I try
     to force you to be.

The train arrives, and we're on,
This generation, the last, and the next beside me –
Adjusting her hair in a mirror, pencilling her dusky eyes,
Then flipping through a glossy magazine and talking
In rapid quickfire, laughing, as I read about you, John.
What is it that suddenly steals over me like a shiver
As I wonder if the whole of this has been wrong?
That I've done nothing, achieved nothing
But a wound of illusion in the heart of it?

I sit with that, feeling – believing it, why not?
Who the hell am I to pretend to anything?
All I've done is indulge a terrible delusion.
All it is is simply infidelity.

The rails curve, blank to passing stations,
And I'm ready to let the whole thing go.
Only show me a sign, show me anything …

When I come off the train, call you and wait,
All I can see is that people's faces are light:
There by the ticket barrier – there at the flower-seller's –
And here at the bus stop where I stand apart.

I glance up and the sky is cloud – cloud, but every kind of cloud:
One like a triangle, another like a floating cross,
One like a curved arch, another like a floating whale

And as you come, smiling, opening the door wide,
The light in your eyes as I lean in to embrace you,
As if you're saying *there's been no mistake.*

We drive out over the bridge; I'm pointing out the sky to you
And we count the shapes of the clouds together,
The clocktower behind us shining gold on blue …

I'm saying it's strange, you know, but it's as if it's all one place:
Iona, London, Stroud – all held by the sky as they are;
We think of them as separate, but it's all one place

It's all one country, it's all One now –

As you welcome me in, we go upstairs,
And the light shines like the sky between us
And there's only one way to be – naked –
Naked as we are as it streams in from the window.

You hold me as you have so many times before.
As our eyes close, I feel you, then the whole of you inside –
And was it all for this? To come back to this? *Yes.*

As I let go with you now, it's all Love,
All of it as the centre opens under us;
It opens like a circle and we're standing in it,
Then its further circles open like ripples
On whiteness-sunlight ground that is green,
All the circles of love there are

                                        nearest and farthest

And we're all in Love and there is no contradiction
With who you love, or who I'm loving,
With whoever we turn to *when we turn to them in love*

– you turning away through the Abbey

                                        leaving me

– your hands waving and fluttering

                                        from the jetty

Then you here as I laugh and cry seeing it

Crying, laughing, shaking

As the downquivers of light become colour, image, body,
All our bodies – all your bodies –

And I don't know whether to laugh or cry – both!
I feel so young and it's only just beginning;

It's the eye of the needle I have come through, with you,
With you under me, in me, oh with me

And I'm shaking my head like a swimmer
And I'm feeling *I don't deserve it* – and I don't –

But you say *let go now*, you're whispering *let go*

And we are fields of love moving everywhere like blossoms,
We are white with love radiating it like seeds

And we are one people – the People of God;
We are all one people now – the People of Love

Closest and farthest doesn't matter;
It's only a difference of degree and not in kind

We are *in You*, Holy Spirit, as you are in us

And I am my name
                    and my name is joy

And I am in my name
                    and my name is Love

    All I can see is circle after circle of love
    – white-centred and interwoven, overlapping like us.
    All I could see was all there is – and it was Love.

Acknowledgements

My deep thanks to all in the Interfaith Pilgrimage group of June–July 1990, especially Tom Gulliver for making it possible; and to Val Denton and Sheila Holloway for being my companions.

The Prison Phoenix Trust, based in Oxford, exists to take meditation into prisons. Ann Wetherall was the sister of my stepmother Tigger (Margaret) Stack.

The brief contextual quotations from Sorley Maclean's 'The Woods of Raasay' are from a *From Wood to Ridge* (Carcanet Press, 1989).

In the Iona sections, the liturgy quotations are from *The Iona Community Handbook* (Wild Goose Publications, 1988). Hymns are from *Hymns Ancient & Modern*.

The map on p. vi is from the World Congress of Faiths flyer for the 1990 Interfaith Pilgrimage. The line by Gabriel Bradford#

Some extracts from this poem (in Days 2, 5, and 14) first appeared in *Kingdom of the Edge* (Element Books, 1999).

Thanks also to Kim Simpson and Jan Angelo for their encouragement in the writing; Anthony Nanson for his brilliant editorial eye and compassionate mind; Kirsty Hartsiosis for her empathic and generous design; and Carole, at the Source, then and now, where time has not stood still.

www.awenpublications.co.uk

Also available from Awen Publications:

Places of Truth:
journeys into sacred wilderness
Jay Ramsay

Poet and psychotherapist Jay Ramsay has been drawn to wild places all his writing life, in search of a particular deep listening experience. 'Trwyn Meditations', a sequence set in Snowdonia, begins this 24-year odyssey. 'By the Shores of Loch Awe' takes us to the fecund wilds of Scotland. 'The Oak' celebrates an ancient tree in the heart of the Cotswolds. 'The Sacred Way' is an evocation of Pilgrim Britain. 'Culbone' records the hidden history of the smallest parish church in England in a steep North Somerset valley near where Coleridge wrote 'Kubla Khan'. The final sequences, 'The Mountain' and 'Sinai', takes us beyond, in all senses, touching the places where we find I and Self.

'Here is a poet who dares the big picture, writing unequivocally from the soul to the soul.' *Alan Rycroft*, Caduceus

Poetry ISBN 978-1-906900-40-3 £12.00 Spirit of Place Volume 4

Iona
Mary Palmer

What do you do when you are torn apart by your 'selves'? The pilgrim poet, rebel Mordec and tweedy Aelia set sail for Iona – a thin place, an island on the edge. It's a journey between worlds, back to the roots of their culture. On the Height of Storm they relive a Viking massacre, at Port of the Coracle encounter vipers. They meet Morrighan, a bloodthirsty goddess, and Abbot Dominic with his concubine nuns. There are omens, chants, curses … During her stay Mordec learns that words can heal or destroy, and the poet writes her way out of darkness. A powerful story, celebrating a journey to wholeness, from an accomplished poet.

Poetry ISBN 978-0-9546137-8-5 £6.99 Spirit of Place Volume 1

Soul of the Earth: the Awen anthology of eco-spiritual poetry
edited by Jay Ramsay

Beautifully crafted, yet challenging received wisdom and pushing boundaries, these are cutting-edge poems from a new generation of writers who share a love of the Earth and haven't given up on humans either. In poems as light as a butterfly and as wild as a storm you'll find vivid, contemporary voices that dare to explore a spiritual dimension to life on Earth and, in doing so, imply that a way out of our global crisis of ecological catastrophe, financial meltdown, and bankruptcy of the spirit is to look beyond the impasse of materialism. With contributions from poets in the USA, Canada, UK, Australia, and New Zealand, this anthology reaches out across the planet to embrace the challenges and blessings of being alive on the Earth in the twenty-first century.

'All real poetry seeks to "renew the face of the earth" – and so to resist the exploiting, banalization or defacing of what lies around us. I hope this collection will serve the renewal of vision we so badly need.'
Most Revd Dr Rowan Williams

Poetry ISBN 978-1-906900-17-5 £12.00

Crackle of Almonds: selected poems
Gabriel Bradford Millar

In these renegade poems ranging from 1958 to 2011 Gabriel Bradford Millar presents a spectrum of life, in all its piquant poignancy, with unfaltering precision, defiance, and finesse. From the very first to the very last, the breathtaking skill of this consummate wordsmith does not waver. Many of the poems linger in the air – not least because Millar performs them orally with such verve. She believes 'that poems, like love-talk, should go from mouth to ear without any paper in between'. On the page their orality and aurality fragrance their presence without diminishing their literary elegance. Continually astonishing, these epicurean poems not only offer a lasting testimony to a 'life well-lived', but inspire the reader to live well too

'She does not just write *about* the world; she dips her syllables in the bitter sweet of its "gazpacho". She thinks melodically.' *Paul Matthews*

Poetry ISBN 978-1-906900-29-8 £9.99

A Dance with Hermes
Lindsay Clarke

In a verse sequence that swoops between wit and ancient wisdom, between the mystical and the mischievous, award-winning novelist Lindsay Clarke elucidates the trickster nature of Hermes, the messenger god of imagination, language, dreams, travel, theft, tweets, and trading floors, who is also the presiding deity of alchemy and the guide of souls into the otherworld. Taking a fresh look at some classical myths, this vivacious dance with Hermes choreographs ways in which, as an archetype of the poetic basis of mind, the sometimes disreputable god remains as provocative as ever in a world that worries – among other things – about losing its iPhone, what happens after death, online scams, and the perplexing condition of its soul.

Poetry/Mythology ISBN 978-1906900-43-4 £10.00

The Immanent Moment
Kevan Manwaring

The sound of snow falling on a Somerset hillside, the evanescence of a waterspout on a remote Scottish island, the invisible view from a Welsh mountain, the light on the Grand Canal in Venice, the fire in a Bedouin camelherder's eyes ... These poems consider the little epiphanies of life and capture such fleeting pulses of consciousness in sinuous, euphonic language. A meditation on time, mortality, transience, and place, this collection celebrates the beauty of both the natural and the man-made, the familiar and the exotic, and the interstices and intimacy of love.

Poetry ISBN 978-1-906900-41-0 £8.99

The Fifth Quarter
Richard Selby

The Fifth Quarter is Romney Marsh, as defined by the Revd Richard Harris Barham in *The Ingoldsby Legends*: 'The World, according to the best geographers, is divided into Europe, Asia, Africa, America and Romney Marsh.' It is a place apart, almost another world. This collection of stories and poems explores its ancient and modern landscapes, wonders at its past, and reflects upon its present. Richard Selby has known Romney Marsh all his life. His writing reflects the uniqueness of The Marsh through prose, poetry, and written versions of stories he performs as a storyteller.

Fiction/Poetry ISBN 978-0-9546137-9-2 £9.99 Spirit of Place Volume 2

Ditch Vision:
essays on poetry, nature, and place
Jeremy Hooker

Ditch Vision is a book of essays on poetry, nature, and place that extends Jeremy Hooker's thinking on subjects that, as a distinguished critic and poet, he has made his life's work. The writers he considers include Edward Thomas, Robert Frost, Robinson Jeffers, Richard Jefferies, John Cowper Powys, Mary Butts, and Frances Bellerby. Through sensitive readings of these and other writers, he discusses differences between British and American writers concerned with nature and spirit of place. The book also includes essays in which he reflects upon the making of his own work as a lyric poet. Written throughout with a poet's feeling for language, *Ditch Vision* is the work of an exploratory writer who seeks to understand the writings he discusses in depth, and to illuminate them for other readers. Hooker explores the 'ground' of poetic vision with reference to its historical and mythological contexts, and in this connection *Ditch Vision* constitutes also a spiritual quest.

Literary Criticism ISBN 978-1906900-51-9 £14.00

Tidal Shift: selected poems
Mary Palmer

Knowing her end was near, Mary Palmer worked on her poems, compiling her very best and writing new ones with a feverish intensity. This is the result, published here with her full cooperation and consent. These are poems from the extreme edge and very centre of life – words of light that defy death's shadow with a startling intensity, clarity, and honesty. Containing poems from across Mary's career, selected by Jay Ramsay, *Tidal Shift* is an impressive legacy from a poet of soul and insight.

'She has the courage to confront struggles and sickness, the world's and her own. Unpious but radically spiritual, she stays faithfully questioning right to the end.' *Philip Gross*

Poetry ISBN 978-1-906900-09-0 £9.99

Lightning Source UK Ltd.
Milton Keynes UK
UKHW03f1821130418
321035UK00001B/28/P

9 781906 900540